TEACHING GUIDE / 2

Silver Burdett Ginn Science
DISCOVERYWORKS

Earth Through Time

Welcome

to Silver Burdett Ginn *Science DiscoveryWorks* – a science program that engages students in active investigations of scientific concepts. *Science DiscoveryWorks* reflects our belief that the best science education for students is one that gradually introduces them to the knowledge, methods, skills, and attitudes of scientists, while simultaneously recognizing and respecting the educational and developmental needs of all students.

Silver Burdett Ginn
Parsippany, NJ   Needham, MA
Atlanta, GA   Irving, TX   Deerfield, IL   Santa Clara, CA

Silver Burdett Ginn
A Division of Simon & Schuster
299 Jefferson Road, P.O. Box 480
Parsippany, NJ 07054-0480

Acknowledgements appear on page C96 which constitutes an extension of this copyright page.

ISBN 0-382-33459-0

3 4 5 6 7 8 9 10 GB 05 04 03 02 01 00 99 98 97 96

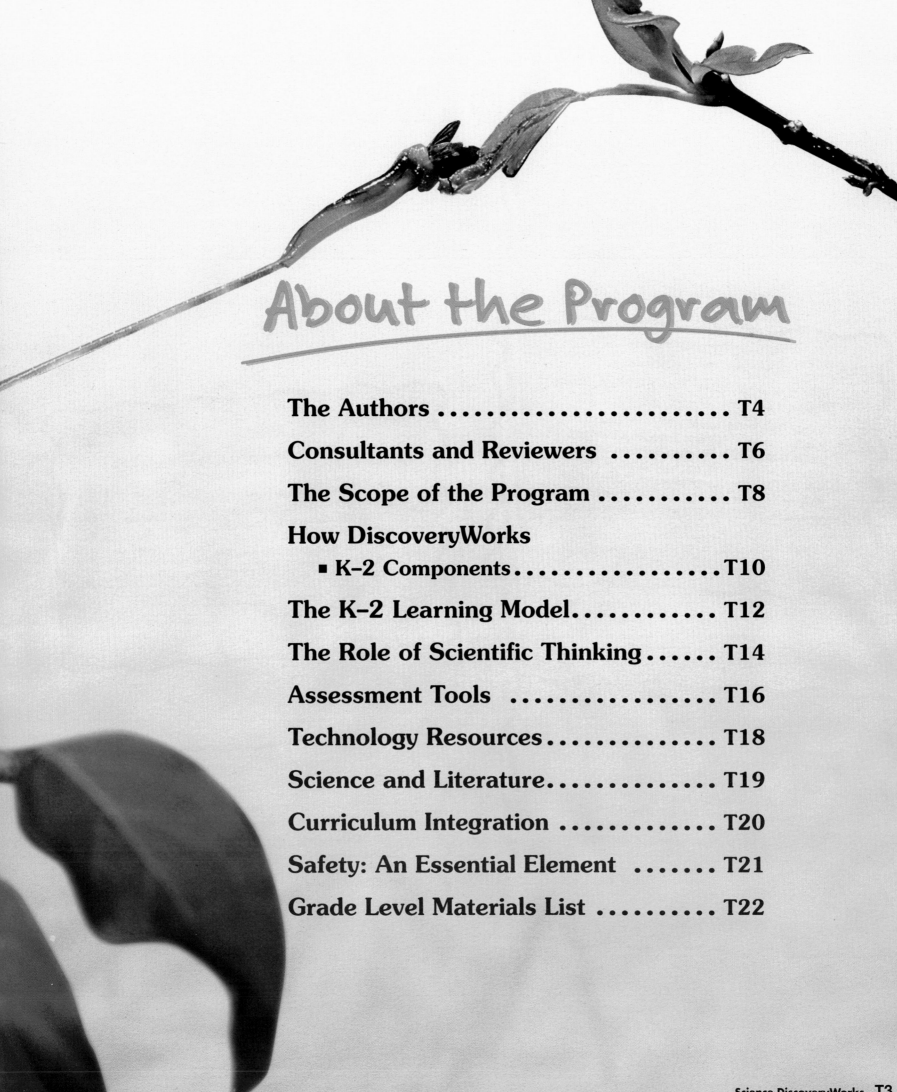

About the Program

THE AUTHORS

Coming from Diverse Backgrounds, Meeting on Common Ground

Mr. William Badders

Science Resource Teacher, Cleveland Public Schools, Cleveland, OH

A 1992 Presidential Awards Winner, Mr. Badders teaches science to students in grades K through 6. He is a member of the Working Group on Science Assessment Standards, a subcommittee of the National Research Council's National Committee on Science Education Standards and Assessment. He specializes in the biological and physical sciences.

Dr. Victoria Fu

Professor of Child Development, Virginia Polytechnic Institute and State University, Blacksburg, VA

Dr. Fu has over twenty years of experience in teaching child development. She has been involved, on the national level, in developing guidelines for appropriate practices, curriculum, and assessment in early childhood programs. She is currently researching and writing papers on how young children construct knowledge.

Dr. Lowell Bethel

Professor of Science Education, The University of Texas at Austin, Austin, TX

Dr. Bethel recently served as Program Director for Teacher Enhancement at the National Science Foundation. He specializes in the biological and physical sciences, urban and multicultural education, constructivism, and the development of learning and teaching models.

Mr. Donald Peck

Director, The Center for Elementary Science, Fairleigh Dickinson University, Madison, NJ

Mr. Peck's extensive experience in science education includes conducting over 500 hands-on science workshops for elementary school teachers. He specializes in the physical and earth sciences.

Dr. Carolyn Sumners

Director of Astronomy & Physics, Houston Museum of Natural Science, Houston, TX

Dr. Sumners directs the museum's Burke Baker Planetarium, the Challenger Learning Center, and the rooftop Brown Observatory and astronomy lab. Her experience includes extensive involvement in the creation and dissemination of science materials and the design and operation of the nation's first Challenger Learning Center. She has a strong background in physics and astronomy.

Ms. Catherine Valentino

Senior Vice President for Curriculum Development Voyager Expanded Learning, West Kingston, RI

Ms. Valentino has experience as a classroom teacher, a curriculum coordinator, and as a director of elementary and secondary education. In her current position, she is specializing in developing materials for after-school programs. She has a background in the biological sciences, particularly in the science of the human body.

CONSULTING AUTHOR

Mr. R. Mike Mullane

Astronaut, retired
Albuquerque, NM

As one of the first mission specialist astronauts, Mr. Mullane logged 356 hours aboard the space shuttles. Now retired from NASA, Mr. Mullane works to bring the experience of spaceflight to "Earthbound" students and adults. He has a strong background in engineering and in the physical sciences.

We believe . . .

As individuals we come from a variety of backgrounds, but, as educators, we meet on common ground. We share a vision of effective science education for all children. Our vision is based on these principles.

Our Principles

- Students learn science concepts most effectively when they explore concrete examples of these concepts. We provide students with many opportunities to construct their own knowledge of science through hands-on activities that are pertinent to the concerns of their daily lives.

- In a world that is growing increasingly dependent on the contributions of science, scientific literacy is an important educational goal for all students. To enable you to help your students achieve this goal, we provide resources that help you respond to the needs of individual students and to the cultural diversity of students.

- Science education is enhanced when based upon reliable educational standards that guide student attainment, curriculum content, and teaching practices. **Science DiscoveryWorks** is based on the *Benchmarks for Science Literacy* prepared by Project 2061, a long-term educational reform project of the American Association for the Advancement of Science, and the *National Science Education Standards* prepared by the National Research Council.

- Students should learn about the big ideas or common themes of science as identified by Project 2061. Four common themes—systems, models, constancy and change, and scale—are used throughout **Science DiscoveryWorks**.

The Authors

CONSULTANTS & REVIEWERS

Lisa Acy
Louis Agassiz Elementary Sch.
Cleveland, OH

Judith Ball
Coordinator for
Math/Science/Health
School District U46
Elgin, IL

Karen R. Bishop
Ferron Elementary School
Ferron, UT

Jean Blackshear
Fred A. Toomer Elementary Sch.
Atlanta, GA

Bonnie Bohrer
Brookview Elementary School
Brook Park, OH

Robert L. Burtch
1990 Presidential Award Winner
Batavia Middle School
Batavia, IL

Martha Christine
Calypso Elementary School
Bethlehem, PA

Mary Eve Corrigan
The Columbus Academy
Gahanna, OH

John S. Detrick
Emeritus Dept. Chair of
Mathematics and Holder of the
McElroy Chair of Mathematics
The Columbus Academy
Gahanna, OH

Robert C. Dixon
National Center to Improve the
Tools of Educators (NCITE)
University of Oregon, College
of Education
Eugene, OR

Denise Pitts-Downing
James Elverson Middle School
Philadelphia, PA

Michaeline A. Dudas
Science and Math Instructional
Support/Consultant
Northbrook, IL

William Dudrow
The Columbus Academy
Gahanna, OH

Barbara Elliott
1990 Presidential Award Winner
Ray E. Kilmer Elementary School
Colorado Springs, CO

Fred Fabry
Retired teacher of Geology
and Biology
Deerfield High School
Deerfield, IL

Rhea Foster
Anderson Park Elementary Sch.
Atlanta, GA

Linda Froschauer
1993 Presidential Award Winner
Weston Middle School
Weston, CT

Joanne Gallagher
Tamarac Middle School
Melrose, NY

Marlene Gregor
Elem. Science Consultant
Bloomington, IL

William L. Handy, Jr.
Parkland School District
Orefield, PA

Beverly Hanrahan
Franconia Elementary School
Souderton, PA

Renee Harris
Northwestern Lehigh Mid. Sch.
New Tripoli, PA

Rhonda Hicks
James Elverson Middle School
Philadelphia, PA

**Sr. Marie Patrice
Hoare, S.L.**
Loretto Middle School
El Paso, TX

**Lester Y. Ichinose,
Ph.D.**
Evanston, IL

Mace A. Ishida, Ph.D.
Diversity and Ed. Consultant
Blacklick, OH

Kristine D. Jackson
Belleville, IL

Pearline A. James
W. F. Slaton Elementary School
Atlanta, GA

Evette Jones
Grover Cleveland Elementary
Philadelphia, PA

Charlene Kalinski
L. L. Hotchkiss Elementary Sch.
Dallas, TX

**Sr. Sharon Kassing,
S.L.**
St. Pius Catholic School
Kirkwood, MO

John Kibler
InterAmerica Intercultural
Training Institute
Des Plaines, IL

Sharon Lempner
R. G. Jones School
Cleveland, OH

Barbara Leonard
1992 Presidential Award Winner
Heritage Elementary School
Pueblo, CO

Gus Liss
Young Elementary School
Burlington Township, NJ

Jo Ann Liss
Intervale School
Parsippany, NJ

Marlenn Maicki
1990 Presidential Award Winner
Detroit Country Day School
Bloomfield Hills, MI

Lynn Malok
Spring Garden Elementary Sch.
Bethlehem, PA

Barbara Mecker
Rockwood South Middle Sch.
St. Louis, MO

Leonardo Melton
Fred A. Toomer Elementary Sch.
Atlanta, GA

Bonnie Meyer
Tremont Elementary School
Cleveland, OH

Dr. Suzanne Moore
L. L. Hotchkiss Elementary Sch.
Dallas, TX

Kathy Morton
Christ the King School
Atlanta, GA

**Dr. Ngoc-Diep T.
Nguyen**
Director, Bilingual and
Multicultural Program
Schaumburg, IL

Michael O'Shea
R. G. Jones School
Cleveland, OH

Wendy Peterson
Harvey Rice Elementary School
Cleveland, OH

Alexandra Pond
Science Coordinator
North Shore School
Chicago, IL

Erika Silverman
Public School 41
Bronx, NY

Christine Spinner
Parma, OH

Jean Ann Strillacci
Kennedy Elementary School
Succasunna, NJ

Laura Swanson
WATTS Intermediate School
Burlington City, NJ

Arthur F. Tobia
Public School 41
Bronx, NY

Nancy Vibeto
1993 Presidential Award Winner
Jim Hill Middle School
Minot, ND

Sandra Wilson
McKinley Elementary School
Abington, PA

Bonita Wylie
Excelsior Middle School
Shorewood, MN

THE SCOPE OF THE PROGRAM
An Overview of Concepts and Themes

	KINDERGARTEN	GRADE 1	GRADE 2
Life Science 	**UNIT A Characteristics of Living Things** Classification of objects as living or non-living; basic needs and stages of growth of living things **Themes:** *Systems, Constancy and Change*	**UNIT A Kinds of Living Things** The similarities and differences between plants and animals; classifying plants and animals according to one characteristic **Theme:** *Systems*	**UNIT A Interactions of Living Things** The needs of living things; plant and animal adaptations to various habitats; the effect of living things, including people, and natural forces on environments **Themes:** *Constancy and Change, Models* 
Physical Science 	**UNIT B Exploring With the Senses** Using the senses to observe the physical characteristics of objects; grouping objects by their physical characteristics **Theme:** *Systems* **UNIT D Pushes and Pulls** Different ways things move; pushes and pulls; surfaces; directional motion **Themes:** *Systems, Models*	**UNIT C Magnets** The properties of magnets; magnetic force; magnetic fields; temporary magnets; magnets and compasses **Themes:** *Systems, Scale* 	**UNIT B Light and Color** Characteristics of light, such as light sources, how light affects vision, and the way light travels; how shadows are formed and changed; the spectrum and color mixing **Theme:** *Systems* **UNIT D Solids, Liquids, and Gases** Properties of solids, liquids, and gases; the changing of materials from one state to another **Theme:** *Constancy and Change*
Earth Science 	**UNIT C Looking at the Sky** Daytime sky and the Sun; differences between the daytime and nighttime sky; the Moon and the stars **Themes:** *Constancy and Change, Scale*	**UNIT B Weather and Seasons** Factors that affect the weather; seasonal weather changes; how people, plants, and animals respond to weather conditions **Theme:** *Constancy and Change* **UNIT D Earth's Land and Water** Properties of soil and rocks; how water and soil mix; how water flows; recycling through composting **Themes:** *Systems, Models*	**UNIT C Earth Through Time** Characteristics of different dinosaurs; how fossil imprints and fossil remains provide clues about the earth's history **Themes:** *Models, Scale, Constancy and Change* 
The Human Body 	**UNIT E Body Parts** Identification of internal and external body parts; the functions and importance of individual body parts, including the hands, bones, muscles, heart, stomach, and brain **Themes:** *Systems, Models*	**UNIT E Keeping Fit and Healthy** The importance of good nutrition, exercise, sleep, and proper hygiene; the food pyramid and a healthful diet **Themes:** *Systems, Constancy and Change*	**UNIT E What Makes Me Sick** How germs cause illness; how illnesses spread; prevention of illnesses and injuries; how to stay healthy **Themes:** *Systems, Scale*

> "The science that all students are expected to learn is defined so that students have sufficient time to develop a deep understanding of essential scientific ideas rather than superficial acquaintance with many isolated facts.
>
> National Science Education Standards

GRADE 3

UNIT A Life Cycles
Stages in the life cycles of animals and plants; changes in animals and plants as they mature; ways that animals and plants survive
Theme: *Models*

UNIT E Roles of Living Things
The needs of living things in relation to their environments; how living things adapt to their environments, change them, and respond to them
Theme: *Constancy and Change*

UNIT C Forms of Energy
The forms of energy and their effect on matter; how heat energy moves, changes matter, and is measured; the benefits and drawbacks of different energy sources
Theme: *Systems*

UNIT B Sun, Moon, and Earth
The physical features of the Sun and Moon; the rotation and revolution of Earth and the Moon; Earth's seasonal changes; eclipses
Theme: *Scale*

UNIT D Earth's Water
Characteristics of Earth's water, including sources of fresh water and the water cycle; water distribution, pollution, and conservation
Theme: *Systems*

UNIT F What's for Lunch?
Nutrients and the types and amounts of food in a healthful diet; sanitary food storage and preparation; care of teeth and gums; digestion
Theme: *Systems*

GRADE 4

UNIT C Animals
Basic needs of animals; adaptations that help animals meet their needs; classification of living things; characteristics of different animal groups
Theme: *Systems*

UNIT B Properties of Matter
Physical properties; states; effects of heat loss or gain and of physical and chemical changes

UNIT D Magnetism and Electricity
Properties of magnets; forms of electrical energy; electric circuits; sources of electric current; how electric current is changed into useful energy
Theme: *Models*

UNIT A Earth's Land Resources
How moving water, wind, and ice shape the land; natural resources and conservation efforts; consequences of producing and disposing of trash
Theme: *Constancy and Change*

UNIT E Weather and Climate
Earth's atmosphere; effects of changes in the air on weather; weather patterns and predictions; seasonal weather changes and climate
Theme: *Constancy and Change*

UNIT F The Body's Delivery Systems
Organs and functions of the respiratory, circulatory, and excretory systems; health measures that prevent or fight disease; harmful effects of nicotine, alcohol, and other drugs
Theme: *Systems*

GRADE 5

UNIT A Plants
Parts of flowering plants; plant cells; plant processes; classifying plants; structural adaptations
Theme: *Systems*

UNIT D Populations and Ecosystems
Dynamic interactions of living and nonliving things in an ecosystem; how energy and matter flow through an ecosystem; biomes; biodiversity
Theme: *Systems*

UNIT C Energy, Work, and Machines
Properties of energy, including its forms, ability to change form, and effects; friction; simple machines
Theme: *Systems*

UNIT F Light and Sound
Properties of light; lenses and their uses; color; properties of sound; the sense of hearing; controlling, recording, and transmitting sound
Theme: *Models*

UNIT B The Solar System and Beyond
The night sky; how astronomers learn about space; the solar system; stars and galaxies; survival in space
Theme: *Scale*

UNIT E The Solid Earth
Properties and uses of minerals and rocks; the rock cycle; Earth's structure; fossils as clues to the age of rocks; the formation of mountains; faults
Theme: *Constancy and Change*

UNIT G Movement and Control
Organs and functions of the skeletal and muscular systems; avoiding bone and muscle injuries; organs and functions of the nervous system; harmful effects of tobacco, alcohol, and other drugs
Theme: *Systems*

GRADE 6

UNIT A Cells and Microbes
Structure and life processes of cells, including mitosis; protists and fungi; bacteria and viruses
Theme: *Models*

UNIT D Continuity of Life
Asexual reproduction; sexual reproduction, including meiosis; inherited and acquired traits; evolution, including evidence for evolution and evolutionary processes
Theme: *Constancy and Change*

UNIT C The Nature of Matter
Physical/chemical properties; elements, compounds, mixtures; physical and chemical changes; acids and bases; atomic structure
Theme: *Scale*

UNIT F Forces and Motion
Characteristics of motion; gravity; measuring changes in motion; friction; action/reaction forces; how forces affect the motion of objects
Theme: *Scale*

UNIT B The Changing Earth
Theory of plate tectonics; the movement of continents; the formation of mountains; earthquakes and volcanoes
Theme: *Models*

UNIT E Oceanography
Contents and properties of ocean water; features and exploration of the ocean floor; currents, waves, and tides; resources from the ocean; ocean pollution
Theme: *Systems*

UNIT G Growing Up Healthy
Human reproduction; the endocrine system and the human life cycle; defenses of the immune system; illness and immune system disorders; reducing health risk factors
Theme: *Systems*

Silver Burdett Ginn Science
How DISCOVERYWORKS
in Grades K-2

The Teaching Guide, Activity Cards, and Poster Book are the key components of each lesson. Choose from additional resources to introduce, extend, and enrich lesson concepts.

Trade Books

Trade Books can be used to introduce the lessons and reinforce concepts.

Teaching Guide

The Teaching Guide shows how the components for each lesson can be used together.

Activity Cards

Activity Cards provide children with opportunities for hands-on explorations.

Science Notebook

Science Notebook pages help children record their observations and conclusions as they work through hands-on explorations. The completed pages can be used as a basis for portfolios.

Assessment

Assessment opportunities are embedded in the components of the lesson.

Additional Resources

A wide range of resources provide additional opportunities for teaching and learning through different modalities.

Choose from these resources:

- Audiotape or CD
- Videotape
- Home-School Connection
- Unit Project
- Assessment Guide
- Science Center Activities
- Lesson Assessment

Poster Book

Large laminated pictures with text and overlays facilitate lively whole group instruction and encourage interaction with the Poster Book.

Picture Cards

Picture Cards extend the Poster Book and can also be used for group or individual work in Science Centers.

K-2 Components

Teaching Guide

Activity Cards

Poster Book

Picture Cards

Trade Books

Teacher Resource Book

    Home-School Connections

    Science Notebook

    Activity Support

    Assessment Guide

    Unit Project Pages

Technology

    Audiotapes or CDs

    Videotapes

Equipment Kits

    Grade Level Kits

    Module Kits

Student Edition

    Grade 1 Book

    Grade 2 Book

A Learning Model for

Silver Burdett Ginn Science
DiscoveryWorks

Setting the Stage

- Read a trade book, use a simple hands-on activity, play an audiotape, or show a videotape to introduce the lesson concept and stimulate interest.

- Assess prior knowledge through discussion of the trade book, activity, audiotape, or videotape.

Using the Activity Card

- Guide students as they work in small groups to explore the lesson concept through the use of an Activity Card and the Equipment Kit.

- Encourage students to discuss their observations, make predictions, and draw conclusions from the activity.

- Have students record their observations and conclusions in their Science Notebooks.

- Assess each student's performance through classroom observation and/or a skills checklist from the Assessment Guide.

Flexibility is an important feature of the components of the **Science DiscoveryWorks** program. Although the Teaching Guide suggests ways in which you can use the program components to organize and guide each lesson, you can adapt these suggestions or develop your own lesson strategies. The model below shows one possible way of organizing a single lesson within a unit.

Using the Poster Book & Picture Cards

- Use the Poster Book and Picture Cards to facilitate lively, whole group instruction and interaction with the visuals.

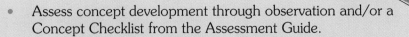

- Encourage students to make and test predictions in response to the Poster Book page.

- Make curricular and cultural connections to the lesson concept using suggestions from the Teaching Guide.

- Assess concept development through observation and/or a Concept Checklist from the Assessment Guide.

Investigate Further

- Have students extend and reinforce their understanding of the concept by completing the In the Science Center Activity.

- Support and guide students as they work on a Unit Project Link.

- Involve families in the learning process with a Home-School Connection activity.

- Make a final assessment of each student's understanding through written and oral activities and the *Science Notebook*.

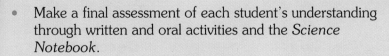

The Role of
SCIENTIFIC THINKING

> *The scientific way of thinking is neither mysterious nor exclusive. The skills involved can be learned by everyone, and once acquired they can serve a lifetime, regardless of one's occupation and personal circumstances.*
>
> *Benchmarks for Science Literacy*

Developing scientific thinking in students is an important part of science education. To learn how to think scientifically, students need frequent opportunities to develop the science process skills, critical thinking skills, and scientific reasoning skills that support scientific inquiry.

In **Science DiscoveryWorks**, students develop process skills as they actively investigate concepts and evaluate the results of their investigations. They develop critical thinking skills and scientific reasoning skills as they respond to thought-provoking questions that conclude every activity and lesson or investigation. In the *Teaching Guide*, questions that promote scientific reasoning skills are identified by this symbol.

The common themes or big ideas that run through science, as well as many other disciplines, are another important aspect of scientific thinking. Common themes are identified for every unit of **Science DiscoveryWorks**, and the connections between the themes and the concepts within a unit are explained in the *Teaching Guide*.

Science Process Skills

Skill	Description
Observing	Determining the properties of an object or event by using the senses
Classifying	Grouping objects or events according to their properties
Measuring/Using Numbers	Skills include: • describing quantitatively using appropriate units of measurement • estimating • recording quantitative data • space or time relationships
Communicating	Using written and spoken words, graphs, tables, diagrams, and other information presentations, including those that are technology based
Inferring	Drawing a conclusion about a specific event based on observations and data; may include cause-and-effect relationships
Predicting	Anticipating consequences of a new or changed situation using past experiences and observation
Collecting, Recording, and Interpreting Data	Manipulating data, either collected by self or by others, in order to make meaningful information and then finding patterns in that information that lead to making inferences, predictions, and hypotheses
Identifying and Controlling Variables	Identifying the variables in a situation; selecting variables to be manipulated and held constant
Defining Operationally	Defining terms within the context of one's own experiences; stating a definition in terms of "what you do" and "what you observe"
Making Hypotheses	Proposing an explanation based on observations
Experimenting	Investigating, manipulating materials, and testing hypotheses to determine a result
Making and Using Models	Representing the "real world" using a physical or mental model in order to understand the larger process or phenomenon

Critical Thinking Skills

Skill	Description
Analyzing	Studying something to identify constituent elements or relationships among elements
Synthesizing	Using deductive reasoning to pull together key elements
Evaluating	Reviewing and responding critically to materials, procedures, or ideas, and judging them by purposes, standards, or other criteria
Applying	Using ideas, processes, or skills in new situations
Generating Ideas	Expressing thoughts that reveal originality, speculation, imagination, a personal perspective, flexibility in thinking, invention, or creativity
Expressing Ideas	Presenting ideas clearly and in logical order, while using language that is appropriate for the audience and occasion
Solving Problems	Using critical thinking skills to find solutions to a problem

Scientific Reasoning Skills

Scientific Reasoning Skill	Description
Longing to Know and Understand	The desire to probe, find information, and seek explanations
Questioning of Scientific Assumptions	The tendency to hold open for further verification presented assumptions, encounters, and ideas
Search for Data and Its Meaning	The propensity to collect information and to analyze it in context
Demand for Verification	The inclination to repeat and replicate findings and studies
Respect for Logic	The inclination to move from assumptions to testing and data collection to conclusions
Consideration of Premises	The tendency to put into context the reason for a particular point of view
Consideration of Consequences	The tendency to put into perspective the results of a particular point of view
Respect for Historical Contributions	The inclination to understand and learn from earlier ideas, studies, and events.

Common Themes*

Theme	Description
Systems	A system is a collection of things that influence one another and appear to be a unified whole. Examples of systems include body systems, the system created as matter and energy interact, and interactions of living and non-living components of ecosystems.
Scale	Ideas concerning the differences in magnitude of variables, such as size, distance, weight, and temperature, including the idea that the properties of something change at different rates as scale changes. Examples of scale include the study of parts of a system, the effects of changing variables in equations, and comparisons of size and distance within systems.
Constancy and Change	The ways in which anything in nature remains the same or changes, as well as the rate at which change occurs. Examples include predator-prey relationships, the idea of conservation of matter and energy, and the continuous cycling of matter and energy in nature.
Models	A model is a physical, mathematical, or conceptual likeness of a thing or process that helps to explain how it works. Models are used to think about processes that happen too slowly, too quickly, or on too large or small a scale to be directly observed. Examples include models of atoms and computer simulations.

*Adapted from _Benchmarks for Science Literacy_ (Oxford University Press, 1993).

ASSESSMENT TOOLS

> *Concepts are learned best when they are encountered in a variety of contexts and expressed in a variety of ways, for that ensures that there are more opportunities for them to become imbedded in a student's knowledge system.*
>
> *Science for All Americans*

In recent years, varied and multiple assessment methods have begun to supplement written tests as the means by which teachers evaluate students' learning. The term *authentic assessment* has been widely used to describe this innovation in education. Authentic assessment is more than a trend that discourages total reliance on written tests. It's actually a new model for teaching and learning that integrates assessment into the learning process.

The following assessment tools are available in **Science DiscoveryWorks.**

- **Lesson Assessments** measure students' understanding of the concept in each lesson.

- **Performance Assessments** evaluate the skills and concepts developed through hands-on activities.

- **Observation and Interview** suggestions and checklists help evaluate and document student's day-to-day progress.

- **Portfolio Assessment** provides a way of demonstrating students' progress over an extended period of time.

- **Self-Assessment** provides a method for students to analyze their own strengths and weaknesses, both individually and in a group.

- **Unit Tests** measure students' understanding and retention of concepts throughout an entire unit.

Performance assessment tools

include Performance Assessment activities, a Process Skills Checklist, and a Group Skills Checklist. They are designed to help you observe and evaluate the ability of students to apply their knowledge of science concepts, skills, and tools, and to work as members of a team. Performance assessment tools are provided for use during hands-on activities and at the end of each unit.

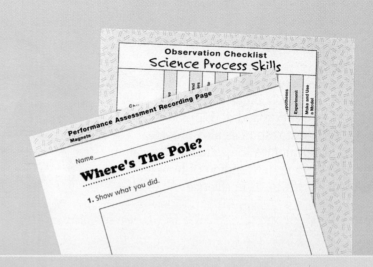

Portfolios

serve as a showcase for a student's best work and provide a way of evaluating the student's progress over time. Portfolio assessment tools include ideas for generating and organizing material for students' portfolios and support materials to help you use portfolios to evaluate each student's progress in science.

Lesson Assessments and Unit Tests

provide a means of assessing students' understanding and retention of important concepts at the end of each lesson and after they have completed an entire unit. A Unit Review appears at the end of each unit in the Student Editions for Grades 1 and 2.

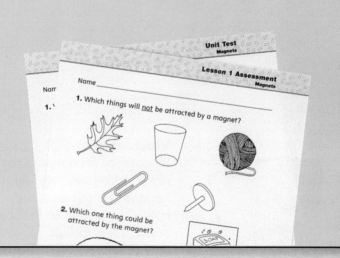

TECHNOLOGY RESOURCES
Extending Our Reach

Science DiscoveryWorks offers a wide variety of technology resources that provide alternative ways of presenting and developing science concepts. These resources also provide students with opportunities to use technological tools and to develop understanding of how technology contributes to advances in science.

The Teaching Guide for each unit of **Science DiscoveryWorks** offers strategies for using the technology resources in lessons or investigations. Suggestions include using technology to introduce a concept, as a stimulus for group discussion, as the basis for an activity or project, and to reinforce a concept.

Technology Resources for Grades K–2

Audiotapes and Compact Discs
The audiotapes and CDs feature a variety of delightful songs that relate to many of the lesson concepts. Students reinforce important concepts as they sing along or pantomime the actions in the songs. One audiotape or CD is available for each grade.

Videotapes
Videotapes present unit concepts in fresh and visually appealing ways; they are both entertaining and educational. Titles include: *Arthur's Eyes, What Good Are Rocks?,* and *Keep the Lights Burning, Abbie.* One videotape is available for each unit; grade level libraries are available.

Technology Resources for Grades 3–6

Science Processor, an Interactive CD-ROM
The CD-ROM Interactive software provides an interactive, child-centered learning approach. The CD-ROM provides Investigations that replace or enhance Investigations in the student book, a Science Workshop in which students can explore and create in an open environment, and a customized encyclopedia. On-screen tools include a Spreadsheet, a Grapher, a Writer, a Painter, a Calculator, and a Timer.

Problem-Solving Videodiscs
The videodiscs use exciting full-motion video, animated diagrams, graphics, and still images to create a captivating learning environment for your students. Each grade-level videodisc contains problems keyed to specific units.

Videotapes
Videotapes that enhance or extend science concepts are suggested on the Using the Power of Technology pages that precede each unit. The videotapes are available from many sources; look for the * to determine which can be ordered from Silver Burdett Ginn.

SCIENCE & LITERATURE
Partners in Learning

In **Science DiscoveryWorks**, literature is used to enhance students' understanding of science concepts. **Science DiscoveryWorks** offers collections of grade-level fiction and non-fiction books that engage students in friendly encounters with the science concepts in each unit of study.

The literary elements of the trade books — imaginative stories, interesting facts, delightful characters, appealing illustrations — have the effect of personalizing science concepts for students. They help connect students' every-day lives to science and heighten their sense of wonder about the natural world.

Trade Books for Grades K–2

A total of ten trade books, two per unit, is available for each grade. The Teaching Guides contain suggestions for integrating the trade books into every lesson. Suggestions include using the trade books to:

- introduce a unit or a lesson concept;

- make a baseline assessment of students' understanding;

- deepen understanding of concepts explored in activities or through the Poster Book;

- stimulate group discussions;

- guide students' independent explorations in the Science Center; and

- prompt student writing about science.

The Teaching Guide also lists other trade books for teachers and for children.

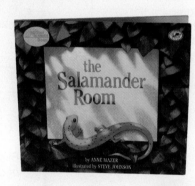

Trade Book Libraries for Grades 3–6

A Trade Book Library, containing a book for each unit, is available for each grade. Highlighted in the Science in Literature features throughout the student editions, the unit trade books provide real-world connections through fictional stories, biographies, and informational genres. The student edition also suggests additional books of interest for each unit that can be used to supplement the Trade Book Library.

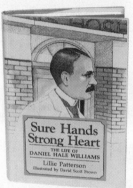

CURRICULUM INTEGRATION
Forming Real Connections

In the **Science DiscoveryWorks** program meaningful connections are made between science and other areas of the curriculum. Science becomes more important to students when they become aware of how fundamental it is to every aspect of their lives. Examples of the types of connections made between science and other areas of the curriculum are shown in the model below.

THE SCIENCES

- Exploring how the areas of Life, Earth, and Physical science are related

LITERATURE

- Using science concepts to explain natural events that occur in a story
- Predicting future events in a story by applying knowledge of science concepts
- Using literature to compare the technology and technological practices of the past and the present

MATH

- Using computational and estimation skills in science activities
- Using different units of measure and measurement tools
- Collecting scientific data and displaying it in graphs

LANGUAGE ARTS

- Writing and illustrating stories and poems
- Exploring the properties of objects that play an important role in a story
- Building vocabulary through an exploration of science terms and related words

CONNECTING SCIENCE TO

CULTURAL CONNECTIONS

- Exploring the natural environments of distant places and the ways in which people have adapted to them
- Exploring the plants and animals of distant places through the literature of other cultures
- Studying the ways in which people from diverse backgrounds have contributed to science

SOCIAL STUDIES

- Studying the ways in which scientific ideas develop over time
- Exploring the influence of social forces on science
- Exploring how geography and natural resources affect the development of science ideas and practices

TECHNOLOGY & SOCIETY

- Exploring the benefits, risks, and limitations of technology
- Relating science concepts to the use of tools and inventions
- Exploring the relationship between science and technology
- Studying the impact of science on society

THE ARTS

- Using music and dance to express science concepts
- Drawing pictures of natural objects and events

SAFETY
An Essential Element

In order for students to develop respect for safety, they need to understand exactly what is meant by safe and unsafe behavior and what the rationale is behind safety rules.

Through your teaching as well as your example, students can develop the "safe science" attitudes and skills that are essential both in school and at home.

General Safety Guidelines

- Post an easy-to-read list of safety rules in a prominent place in the classroom. Review it with students on a regular basis.

- Become familiar with the safety procedures that are necessary for each activity before introducing it to your students.

- Discuss specific safety precautions with students before beginning every hands-on science activity.

- Always act as an exemplary model of safe behavior.

- Have students wear protective aprons, goggles, and gloves whenever these items will prevent injury.

- Keep safety equipment, such as fire blankets and fire extinguishers, readily accessible and know how to use it.

- Prepare students for emergencies by having them practice leaving the classroom quickly and safely.

- Show students how to obtain help in an emergency by using the telephone, an intercom, or other available means of communication.

- Never leave students unattended while they are involved in science activities.

- Provide ample space for science activities that require students to move about and handle materials.

- Keep your classroom and all science materials in proper condition. Check their condition regularly.

- Tell students to report all injuries to you immediately.

For more detailed information on safety, you may wish to order the NSTA publication *Safety in the Elementary Science Classroom* (1993). Write or call the National Science Teachers Association, NSTA Publication Sales, 1840 Wilson Boulevard, Arlington, VA 22201-3000; telephone: (703) 243-7100 or (800) 722-6782.

MATERIALS LIST

Interactions of Living Things 2A

Materials	Quantity for 6 groups of 4	In Kit	C/NC*	Page
aloe	1 to 2		C	A82
ant farm kit	1	✔	NC	A50
ants coupon	1 coupon	✔	C	A50
Aquaria, Super with lid (7 L)	1	✔	NC	A26
bag, paper grocery	6		C	A18
books	5 to 6		NC	A66, A74
bowl, clear plastic (8" diameter × 4")	1	✔	NC	A82
cactuses, small	5 to 6		C	A82
clay, modeling ($1/4$ lb stick)	6 sticks	✔	C	A66
container, large plastic (40 oz)	6	✔	NC	A58
cup, plastic measuring (8 oz)	1	✔	NC	A50
goggles	6	✔	NC	A26, A50, A58, A66, A74, A82
gravel	two 2-lb bags	✔	C	A26, A82
hand lens	15	✔	NC	A18, A34, A42, A82, A90
living animals	10 to 15		C	A26
pan, large foil roasting	2 pkg of 6	✔	NC	A66, A74
paper towels	1 roll		C	A34
peanuts, foam	6 pkg of 15	✔	NC	A58
plants, small	1 flat of 36		C	A74
plants, terrarium	4 to 5		C	A26
objects, bag of woodland	6	✔	NC	A18
rice, uncooked white	1 lb bag	✔	C	A58
sand	1 lb bag	✔	C	A82
seeds, radish	1 pkg	✔	C	A34
soil	nine 4-qt bags	✔	C	A26, A66, A74, A82
sow bugs (isopods)	1 coupon	✔	C	A42
spoon, plastic slotted 11"	6	✔	NC	A58
spray bottle	1 pkg of 2	✔	NC	A42
towel, large	6		NC	A66, A74
tray, aluminum (8" × 12")	1 pkg of 6	✔	NC	A34
tweezers	6	✔	NC	A34, A58
twigs, paper lunch bag full	6		C	A66
water	source		C	A26, A34, A42, A58, A66, A74, A82
water, bottled	$3/4$ cup		C	A50
watering can	6		NC	A26, A66, A74, A82
wood, piece of natural with bark	6		NC	A58
wood, $1/2$" slab with bark	1	✔	C	A42

Light and Color 2B

Materials	Quantity for 6 groups of 4	In Kit	C/NC*	Page
aluminum foil (9" × 12")	1 roll	✔	C	B50
bag, paper grocery	24		C	B26
ball, plastic-foam (1$1/2$")	6	✔	C	B66
battery, AA	12	✔	C	B26, B42, B50, B66, B74, B82
clay, modeling	1-lb box	✔	NC	B66
cloth, black (8" square)	12 pieces	✔	NC	B34
crayons	6 boxes		C	B18, B26, B74, B82
cups, clear plastic (9 oz)	2 pkgs of 25	✔	C	B50, B82
flashlight, AA, water resistant	6	✔	NC	B26, B42, B50, B66, B74, B82
food coloring	1 pkg of 4 colors	✔	C	B82
ice cubes	12		C	B34
index cards, 5" x 8", unlined	1 pkg of 50	✔	C	B26
jar, clear plastic , 16 oz	6	✔	NC	B74

*C/NC = Consumable/Nonconsumable

markers, broad . . . . .6 boxes . . . . .C .B18, B26
milk . . . . .1¹/₂ tsp . . . . .C B50, B74, B82
mirror, plastic (3" x 5") . . . . .6 . . . . ✔ . . .NC B50, B74
newspaper (9" x 12") . . . . .6 sheets . . . . .C .B50
newsprint, large sheet . . . . .6 . . . . .C .B66
objects, bag of small opaque . . . . .1 . . . . .NC .B58
overhead projector . . . . .1 . . . . .NC .B58
pans, aluminum pie, 9" . . . . .12 . . . . . . ✔ . . .NC .B34
paper, construction (9"×12") . . . . .1 pkg of 30 . . . . ✔ . . .C .B50
paper, tissue (9"×12") . . . . .2 pkg of 5 . . . . . ✔ . . .C .B50
paper, waxed . . . . .1 roll . . . . ✔ . . .C .B50
paper, white (11"× 17") . . . . .6 . . . . .C .B82
pencil, sharpened . . . . .6 . . . . .NC .B66
plastic wrap, clear (9"×12") . . . . .1 roll . . . . ✔ . . .C .B50
posterboard (11"×17") . . . . .8 sheets . . . . .C B42, B58, B74
scissors . . . . .6 . . . . .NC B42, B50, B58
stopwatch, digital . . . . .1 . . . . ✔ . . .NC .B34
tape, cellophane . . . . .6 rolls . . . . ✔ . . .C .B26
water . . . . .source . . . . .C . . . . .B50, B74 ,B82

Earth Through Time 2C

Materials	Quantity for 6 groups of 4	In Kit	C/NC*	Page
airtight container	6		NC	C48
blocks of wood (2"×3"×1/2")	12	✔	NC	C66
bones, plastic chicken	6 sets	✔	NC	C58
bones, plastic rat	6 sets	✔	NC	C58
cereal, dry	6 cups		C	C66
crayons or colored pencils	6 boxes		C	C74
dinosaur models with guide	2 sets	✔	NC	C18
dough compound	2 pkgs	✔	C	C42
flour	15 lb		C	C50
fossil imprint of fern	6	✔	NC	C34
fossil imprint of leaf	6	✔	NC	C42
fossil remains of snail	6	✔	NC	C34
goggles	6	✔	NC	C42, C50, C58, C66
golf tees	2 pkg (20)	✔	NC	C66
hand lens	15	✔	NC	C18, C34, C42
measuring cup	1		NC	C50
mixing bowl, large	1		NC	C50
mixing spoon	1		NC	C50
newspapers	several copies		C	C58
once-living object (leaf)	6		C	C42
once-living object (shell)	6	✔	NC	C42
once-living object (twig)	6		C	C42
overhead projector	1		NC	C26
paper plates, large	1 pkg (30)	✔	C	C50, C58
plastic wrap	1		C	C50
ruler, 12"	6		NC	C50
salt	15 cups		C	C50
sand	six 5-lb bags	✔	C	C58
spoons, plastic	12	✔	NC	C58
tape, transparent	6 rolls		C	C74
timer, 1-minute	6	✔	NC	C66
tray, foil	6	✔	NC	C58
tree leaves	12		C	C66
water	1 gallon		C	C50
yardstick	1		NC	C26

*C/NC = Consumable/Nonconsumable

Solids, Liquids, and Gases 2D

Materials	Quantity for 6 groups of 4	In Kit	C/NC*	Page
bag, plastic (11" × 14")	10	✔	NC	D42
bag, plastic (14" × 20")	10	✔	NC	D42
bag, plastic (18" × 40")	10	✔	NC	D42
ball (2" diameter)	6	✔	NC	D18
bottle, squeezable empty plastic (8 oz)	6	✔	NC	D50
button, round	6	✔	NC	D18
cola	6 cups		C	D26
container, clear plastic (6 liter)	6	✔	NC	D50
container, plastic	6	✔	NC	D66, D82
counter, round	6	✔	NC	D18
cups, clear plastic (9 oz)	50	✔	C	D26, D34, D50, D58, D66, D82, D90
food coloring, green	2 bottles	✔	C	D26, D90
gelatin, unflavored	4 boxes	✔	C	D90
goggles	6	✔	NC	D26, D90
ice cubes	6 trays		C	D58, D74
jar, short wide plastic (16 oz)	6	✔	NC	D34, D74, D90
jar, tall thin plastic (12 oz)	6	✔	NC	D34
lid, round jar	6	✔	NC	D18
marble, large	6	✔	NC	D18, D34, D50
metal, rectangular piece (2" × 6")	6	✔	NC	D18
oil, corn	6 cups		C	D26
oil, vegetable	6 cups		C	D26
orange juice	6 cups		C	D26
pan, aluminum pie (9" diameter)	6	✔	NC	D74
paper clips, jumbo	1 box	✔	NC	D18
paper towels	1 roll		C	D26, D34
pencil, grease	6	✔	C	D50, D66, D82
plastic, rectangular piece (2" × 6")	6	✔	NC	D18
plastic wrap	1 roll	✔	C	D66
seltzer water	6 cups		C	D26
tape, masking	1 roll	✔	C	D66
ties, twist	25	✔	C	D42
water	source		C	D26, D34, D50, D66, D74, D82, D90
wood, rectangular piece (2" × 6")	6	✔	NC	D18

What Makes Me Sick 2E

Materials	Quantity for 6 groups of 4	In Kit	C/NC*	Page
candy, stick	8 pieces	✔	C	E34
chalk, red	12 sticks	✔	C	E34
clay (1 lb box)	2 boxes	✔	C	E18
cotton swabs	1 box	✔	C	E34
crayons	6 boxes		C	E58, E66
cup, plastic (9 oz)	25	✔	NC	E34
goggles	6	✔	NC	E34
hand lens	15	✔	NC	E42
hole punch	1		NC	E42
index card, 3" × 5"	100	✔	C	E42
magazines	12 to 24		C	E66
markers	6 boxes		C	E66
paper towels	1 roll		C	E26
petroleum jelly	1 jar	✔	C	E42
plastic, sheet (8 1/2" × 11")	10		NC	E26
plate, large paper (9 in.)	30	✔	C	E18, E34
spray bottle	6	✔	NC	E26
string	1 roll	✔	C	E42
tissues	1 box	✔	C	E26
water	source		C	E26, E34
waxed paper	1 roll	✔	C	E42

*C/NC = Consumable/Nonconsumable

TEACHER NOTES

Teacher Notes

CONTENTS

LESSON 1

INVESTIGATING CHARACTERISTICS OF DINOSAURS . . . **C16**

Concept: *Dinosaurs, which lived on land long ago, had many different characteristics.*

LESSON 2

INVESTIGATING SIZES OF DINOSAURS **C24**

Concept: *Fossils provide evidence that some dinosaurs were among the largest animals that have ever lived and that others were quite small.*

UNIT C

EARTH THROUGH TIME

Unit Overview

In *Earth Through Time,* children learn that dinosaurs lived on the earth millions of years ago and had many different characteristics. Children investigate fossil remains and fossil imprints, developing an understanding of the information fossils can give us about past life on the earth. Finally, children compare dinosaurs to animals living today, find out how animals become extinct, and develop an awareness of the need to protect endangered species.

Unit at a Glance

Lessons	Concepts	Objectives
1 Investigating Characteristics of Dinosaurs, pp. C16–C23 Pacing: 55 minutes	Dinosaurs, which lived on land long ago, had many different characteristics.	**Compare** the characteristics of different types of dinosaurs. **Conclude** that dinosaurs were animals that lived on land a long time ago.
2 Investigating Sizes of Dinosaurs, pp. C24–C31 Pacing: 55 minutes	Fossils provide evidence that some dinosaurs were among the largest animals that have ever lived and that others were quite small.	**Compare** the sizes of dinosaurs to a child's size. **Compare** the sizes of dinosaurs to other objects that the children estimate to be the same size as the dinosaurs.
3 Investigating Kinds of Fossils, pp. C32–C39 Pacing: 55 minutes	Some fossils are the remains of once-living things; some fossils are imprints of once-living things.	**Compare** fossil imprints with fossil remains.
4 Investigating Imprints, pp. C40–C47 Pacing: 55 minutes	A fossil imprint is formed when a plant or animal leaves a trace, or print, of itself in soil, which gradually turns to rock.	**Compare** imprints of common objects with a fossil imprint. **Conclude** that fossil imprints are traces of plants or animals.
5 Investigating Handprints and Footprints, pp. C48–C55 Pacing: 55 minutes	Dinosaur fossil footprints are clues to the size of a dinosaur and the size and shape of its feet.	**Infer** the sizes of people from imprints of their hands. **Conclude** that dinosaur fossil footprints give clues about the sizes of dinosaurs.
6 Investigating Fossil Remains, pp. C56–C63 Pacing: 55 minutes	Fossil bones give clues to sizes and shapes of dinosaurs.	**Infer** the size of an animal from its remains. **Model** scientific behavior by digging up buried remains.
7 Investigating Kinds of Teeth, pp. C64–C71 Pacing: 55 minutes	Flat teeth are good for grinding food, and pointed teeth are good for tearing food.	**Compare** the shapes of teeth that are good for grinding plant matter with teeth that are good for tearing meat. **Conclude** that dinosaur teeth give us clues to what they ate.
8 Investigating Dinosaur Skeletons, pp. C72–C79 Pacings: 55 minutes	Skeletons are clues to sizes and shapes of dinosaurs.	**Assemble** a dinosaur skeleton. **Infer** the shape of a dinosaur from its skeleton.
9 Investigating Dinosaurs and Living Animals, pp. C80–C87 Pacing: 55 minutes	Although dinosaurs became extinct a long time ago, some of them had characteristics similar to animals that are alive today.	**Compare** dinosaurs with living animals. **Conclude** that some animals alive today are in danger of becoming extinct.

Science Themes

To scientists, themes are overarching concepts that can be used to help them see common links among objects or situations that at first appear to be quite different from one another.

MODELS and SCALE Models help children learn by reproducing aspects of the real world on a smaller scale. In *Earth Through Time,* children examine, assemble, and create models of dinosaurs and fossils, distinguish between actual size and scaled-down size, and make size comparisons.

CONSTANCY AND CHANGE Constancy and change refer to two natural varying forces working in an evolutionary balance. In *Earth Through Time,* children note both resemblances and differences in the animals of today compared with the dinosaurs.

Hands-on Science

Unit Resources

Activities	Process Skills	Materials	Advance Preparation
Examining Dinosaur Models	Use models, Observe	Dinosaur models, hand lens	None
Comparing Sizes of Dinosaurs	Measure; Collect, record, and interpret data	Yardstick, overhead projector, dinosaur pictures	Make transparencies from Activity Support blackline masters. Arrange to use the gymnasium and a projector.
Examining Fossils	Communicate; Collect, record, and interpret data	2 fossils, hand lens	None
Comparing Imprints	Make a model, Observe	Goggles, dough, paper plates, once-living objects, fossil imprint	Collect leaves, twigs, and other once-living objects ahead of time.
Comparing Handprints	Make and use models, Measure	Goggles, dough, 12" ruler, paper plates, mystery handprint	Prepare balls of dough needed for children's handprints and mystery handprints. Have mystery handprints made and marked for identification.
Finding Remains in Sand	Collect, record, and interpret data; Observe	Goggles, newspapers, tray, sand, spoons, bones, paper plates	Prepare a tray of sand with hidden bones for each group.
Comparing Kinds of Teeth	Use models, Experiment, Predict	Goggles, tree leaves, golf tees, blocks of wood, timer, dry cereal	Collect tree leaves or plant leaves ahead of time. Cover the work surface with newspapers.
Assembling a Dinosaur Skeleton	Observe, Make and use a model, Infer	Tape, dinosaur skeleton pieces	Copy Activity Support blackline masters and cut out the skeleton pieces. Keep the skeleton pieces of each dinosaur separate.
Comparing Dinosaurs and Living Animals	Classify, Infer	Dinosaur cards, living-animal cards	Copy Activity Support blackline masters. Glue these cards to sturdy index cards, posterboard, or heavy construction paper before cutting them out.

Poster Book and Picture Cards

Student Edition

Activity Cards

Trade Books

Teacher Resource Book
- *Home-School Connection*
- *Science Notebook*
- *Activity Support*
- *Assessment Guide*
- *Unit Project Pages*

Equipment Kit

Videotape

Audiotape or CD

SCIENCE BACKGROUND

eople have long been fascinated with fossils. Since the time of the ancient Greeks and likely before, the nature and meaning of prehistoric remains has intrigued people. Today, scientists who study fossil plants and animals are known as paleontologists. They are interested in determining how life on the earth has developed and changed through time. Paleontologists also try to reconstruct the environments in which living things existed long ago and to compare those environments and life forms with modern environments and life forms.

At present the scientifically accepted estimate for the age of the earth is about 4.5 billion years. A lack of fossils and other evidence prevents us from knowing much about the earliest times. The geological record from about 600 million years ago to the present, is fairly well known. This time period involves changes in the shapes, locations, and climates of the earth's continents and oceans, as well as changes in the forms of life on the planet. One era that is very interesting to many people is the Mesozoic Era, because dinosaurs were the dominant land animals at that time. The Mesozoic Era spans from 225 million years ago to about 65 million years ago. It contains three smaller time periods, the Triassic, the Jurassic, and the Cretaceous.

Dinosaurs have captured the imaginations of young and old alike since skeletal remains began to be sought in earnest during the 1800s. Because their skeletons bring to life such fantastic beasts, dinosaurs have been romanticized, misinterpreted, and misrepresented. Only recently have paleontologists decided that some of the dinosaurs were probably warm-blooded. Some were also cold-blooded, as are reptiles we see today. Some were fast-moving herd animals who parented their young for some time after hatching instead of abandoning eggs after laying. These recent interpretations show how the science of paleontology changes its views to give the most reasonable answers based on the best available evidence and information.

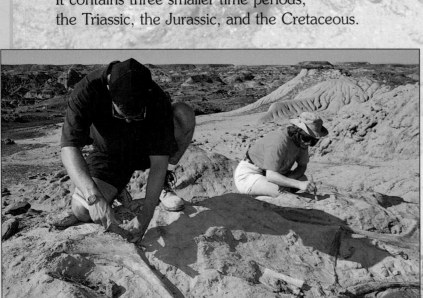

As wonderful as they are, dinosaurs must be viewed with the proper perspective. They were the dominant land animals for a while but then became extinct, along with many other land- and ocean-dwelling life forms, including plants. It appears that such cycles are not the exception but the rule throughout our planet's history. Other types of plants and animals were dominant for a time, became extinct, and were replaced by a succeeding group of organisms. Life on the earth today contains many living things, some of which have appeared recently (modern humans emerged on the earth only about 100,000 years ago), and some that have existed for many millions of years. Paleontologists continue to search for fossils as clues to the history of the earth, not only to better understand the past but also to understand more about the present.

BOOKS FOR TEACHERS

The Big Beast Book by Jerry Booth (Little, Brown, 1988). An introduction to dinosaurs, with instructions for related projects and activities.

....

Fossil by Paul D. Taylor (Knopf, 1990). The photo-essay approach introduces different types of fossils, from bacteria and algae to birds, dinosaurs, and mammals—even "living fossils." The clear photographs practically leap off the page.

....

The Great Dinosaur Atlas by William Lindsay (Julian Messner, 1991). Features less commonly recognized dinosaurs from around the world, using illustrations, maps, and artists' drawings of artifacts, scientists, and equipment.

....

NatureScope: Digging Into Dinosaurs edited by Judy Braus (National Wildlife Federation/The Sewall Company, 1985). A sourcebook of versatile project ideas, activity suggestions, and background information for exploring the world of dinosaurs. Combines science activities with language arts, geography, math, social studies, and arts-and-crafts projects.

....

Water, Stones, and Fossil Bones edited by Karen K. Lund (National Science Teachers Association, 1991). Contains a variety of challenging, teacher-tested earth science activities for elementary and intermediate grades. A separate chapter deals with fossils and the earth's past.

TEACHER Tips

FOSSILS make intriguing long-term displays in the classroom—a great way to reinforce ideas learned from previous lessons and activities.

TRY THIS:

I collect rocks and fossils and leave them scattered around the classroom, along with magnifying glasses and art supplies. During free time, children are encouraged to examine the objects for texture, shapes, size, and other features and to make a visual record of their observations.

Mary Jane Matejka, St. Louis, Missouri

Children enjoy imagining the everyday lives of animals who lived long ago. Following the activity, children can share their ideas and discuss them.

TRY THIS:

I bring in labeled pictures of dinosaurs or a chart of dinosaur names and faces. Each child chooses one dinosaur and draws a picture of the dinosaur in the setting where the animal could live. Alternatively, children write a few sentences about their dinosaur's everyday activities.

Mary Eve Corrigan, Columbus, Ohio

SCIENCE & LITERATURE

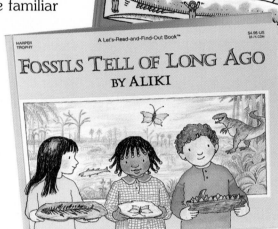

Using the Trade Books

How Big Were the Dinosaurs? by Bernard Most (Harcourt Brace & Company, 1994). Describes the sizes of dinosaurs by comparing them with more familiar objects such as a toothbrush, a school bus, a supermarket, a park bench, and a bowling alley. Use to introduce the unit in Lesson 1 and to enhance children's understanding of concepts presented in Lessons 2, 5, 6, 7, 8, and 9.

Fossils Tell of Long Ago by Aliki (HarperCollins, 1990). Explains how fossils are formed and what they tell us about the history of the earth. Also tells how to simulate a fossil imprint. Use to enhance children's understanding of concepts presented in Lessons 3, 4, and 5.

Other Books for Children | Suggestions for Use

Digging Up Dinosaurs by Aliki (Harper & Row, 1988). Briefly introduces various types of dinosaurs whose skeletons are seen in museums and explains how scientists work with fossilized bones. (PreK–Grade 3)

In Lesson 3: Use with Activity Card C3 to provide more information on the work done by paleontologists.
In Lesson 8: Use with Activity Card C8 to provide further information on dinosaur skeletons.

Dinosaur Bones by Aliki (Crowell, 1988). Discusses how scientists, studying fossil remains, provide information on how dinosaurs lived millions of years ago. (PreK–Grade 3)

In Lesson 4: Use with Activity Card C4 and Poster Book page C4 to reinforce concepts about imprint fossils.
In Lesson 5: Use with Poster Book page C5 to provide additional information on dinosaur footprints.

Dinosaurium by Barbara Brenner (Bantam, 1993). Describes a museum tour through the Triassic, Jurassic, and Cretaceous Periods with information about names and habitats of dinosaurs. (PreK–Grade 3)

In Lesson 1: Read aloud to provide more information on characteristics of dinosaurs.
In Lesson 8: Use with Poster Book page C8 to provide information on the clues provided by dinosaur skeletons.

Janice VanCleave's Dinosaurs for Every Kid: Easy Activities That Make Science Fun by Janice VanCleave (John Wiley, 1994). Interesting activities related to concepts presented in the unit. (Grades 2–5)

In Lesson 2: Use with Poster Book page C2 to provide more information on sizes of dinosaurs.
In Lesson 3: Use with Activity Card C3 to explore different kinds of fossils.

The Magic School Bus: In the Time of the Dinosaurs by Joanna Cole (Scholastic, 1994). Ms. Frizzle's class goes back in time to the dinosaurs to discover adventure and interesting facts. (PreK–Grade 3)

In Lesson 6: Use with Activity Card C6 for additional examples of fossil remains, including eggs and nests.
In Lesson 7: Use with Poster Book page C7 for more information on dinosaur teeth.

Exploring the Videotape

Digging Up Dinosaurs (Reading Rainbow). To get children thinking about dinosaurs, this entertaining film opens with footage from an animated dinosaur movie and a cartoon dinosaur telling jokes. (Comedian Jerry Stiller is the voice of this comic dinosaur.) Host LeVar Burton sets off in his four-wheel-drive "Jeeposaurus Wreck" to explore the mystery surrounding the life and death of these prehistoric creatures. He helps children get a sense of just how large some dinosaurs were and the sounds they might have made by visiting a construction site, where large machinery dwarfs human beings, moves laboriously, and makes loud noises. Then Burton goes to the Dinosaur National Monument in Utah, where dinosaur bones can be found exactly as nature preserved them. The video includes children's reviews of other related books. Use with Lessons 1, 6, and 9.

Using the Audiotape or CD

The *Grade 2 Science Songs* audiotape or CD offers a variety of songs for children to enjoy while it provides enhancement for some of the lesson concepts. The songs can be played before appropriate lessons as an introduction to the concept, or at the end of a lesson as a follow-up activity. Invite children to sing along, or have them pantomime the actions in the songs. The song suggested for this unit is "Dinosaur Tango" (Lessons 1, 2, and 8).

Other Technology Resources

VIDEOTAPES

How Big Were the Dinosaurs? (Coronet QV-491C) Visiting an archaeological dig and a museum, Wondercat learns about fossils and dinosaurs. Comparisons with modern animals provide children with an understanding of extinct creatures and an appreciation of what it means for a species to be endangered. (Lessons 2, 5, 7, 8, 9)

A Magical Field Trip to a Dinosaur Museum. (AIMS) Chris, Nicole, and Rosie visit a museum and a dig site to learn more about dinosaurs and the work of paleontologists. (Lessons 4, 6, 8)

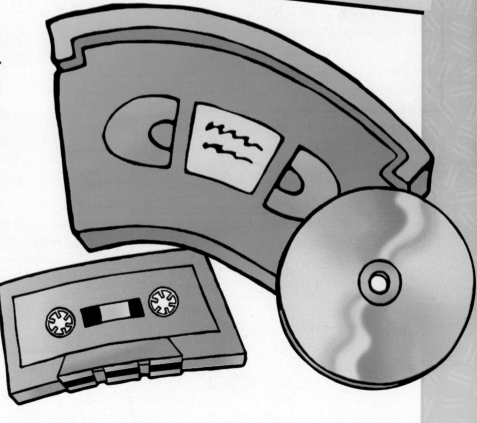

Curriculum INTEGRATION

The exploration of scientific ideas and phenomena is most meaningful when children can see how science is integrated in their lives. Connecting the study of science with other areas of the curriculum helps children see the relationship between science and their lives. The chart indicates the location in the unit of each of these kinds of connections.

LITERATURE

- *How Big Were the Dinosaurs?*, pages C17, C25, C44, C49, C57, C63, C65, C73, C79, C81
- *Fossils Tell of Long Ago*, pages C33, C39, C41, C49

THE SCIENCES

- Exploring Rocks, page C45

MATH

- Measuring Length, page C21
- Counting Years, page C23
- Making a Graph, page C29
- Comparing Animals, page C31
- Graphing Data, page C55
- Measuring Bones, page C61
- Measuring, page C77

CONNECTING SCIENCE TO

LANGUAGE ARTS

- Describing Dinosaurs, page C21
- Telling a Story, page C39
- Writing About Bones, page C61
- Using Words, page C69
- Writing a Letter, page C71
- Writing an Essay, page C85

CULTURAL CONNECTIONS

- Sharing Data, page C37
- Sharing Fossils, page C47

TECHNOLOGY & SOCIETY

- Interpreting Data, page C45

SOCIAL STUDIES

- Using a Scale, page C29
- Drawing a Map, page C53
- Using a Map, page C79
- Sharing Ideas, page C85

ART

- Sculpting With Clay, page C37
- Drawing Remains, page C63
- Sculpting Teeth, page C69
- Making Models, page C77
- Making a Collage, page C87

MUSIC

- Imagining Sounds, page C53

UNIT PROJECT

Dinosaur Place

Children draw dinosaurs and plants to create a Dinosaur Place exhibit that demonstrates their understanding of lesson concepts learned in the Earth Through Time *unit.*

Getting Ready

Grouping

Small groups or individuals

Materials

- Bulletin-board paper and tagboard
- Crayons or colored pencils
- Construction paper
- Scissors
- String and tape
- Raw potatoes
- Metal spoons
- Tempera paint
- Unit Project pages (Teacher Resource Book)

Overview

Children make a Dinosaur Place exhibit. First they make a classroom dinosaur chart and then start their drawings of dinosaurs, dinosaur tracks, food eaten by dinosaurs, and scenery to show the environment. These drawings are mounted on construction paper or tagboard, cut out, and then displayed around the classroom with string and tape. The exhibit also includes children's drawings of dinosaurs and living animals that have similar characteristics. When the Dinosaur Place exhibit is complete, children invite other classes to visit it.

Using the Unit Project Links

Lesson 1 Children make a chart listing characteristics of various dinosaurs. The chart becomes part of the Dinosaur Place exhibit. *See Unit Project Link, page C22.*

Lesson 2 Children make dinosaur pictures which they color, mount, cut out, and display with string and tape. *See Unit Project Link, page C30.*

Lesson 5 Children make dinosaur footprint stamps with raw potatoes. They stamp the dinosaur tracks on bulletin-board paper and label them for display in the exhibit. *See Unit Project Link, page C54.*

Lesson 7 Children draw and mount pictures of plants and animals that dinosaurs might have eaten for food. They also draw trees and volcanoes to include as part of the environment. *See Unit Project Link, page C70.*

Lesson 9 Children draw pictures of dinosaurs and living animals with similar characteristics. They mount the drawings on construction paper to display them in Dinosaur Place. *See Unit Project Link, page C86.*

ASSESSMENT OPTIONS

uthentic assessment options embedded throughout the lessons require children to think critically, solve problems, apply the process of scientific inquiry, and work cooperatively to solve problems.

The table below shows points during the lesson where ongoing assessment occurs. Assess Prior Knowledge sets up a baseline for comparison at the end of the lesson. Assess Performance checks children's use of process skills and group skills, while Assess Concept Development checks their understanding of concepts. Make a Final Assessment returns to the baseline assessment and offers additional authentic assessment options.

Lesson	Assess Prior Knowledge	Assess Performance	Assess Concept Development	Make a Final Assessment
1	page C17	page C19	page C21	page C23
2	page C25	page C27	page C29	page C31
3	page C33	page C35	page C37	page C39
4	page C41	page C43	page C45	page C47
5	page C49	page C51	page C53	page C55
6	page C57	page C59	page C61	page C63
7	page C65	page C67	page C69	page C71
8	page C73	page C75	page C77	page C79
9	page C81	page C83	page C85	page C87

Classroom Observation

Tips for using the observation checklists to record individual and class observations are provided in the Teacher Resource Book.

Lesson Assessment

After exploring the Poster Book page in each lesson, use the Lesson Assessment to evaluate children's understanding of the lesson concept.

Unit Test

When children have finished exploring the unit concepts, you may wish to have them take the Unit Test.

Performance Assessment

When children have finished exploring the unit concepts, you may wish to have them do the Performance Assessment. In this assessment they are asked to make fossils of modern objects, using clay and plaster, and compare them to real fossils. Sample responses and a scoring rubric are provided in the Assessment Guide in the Teacher Resource Book.

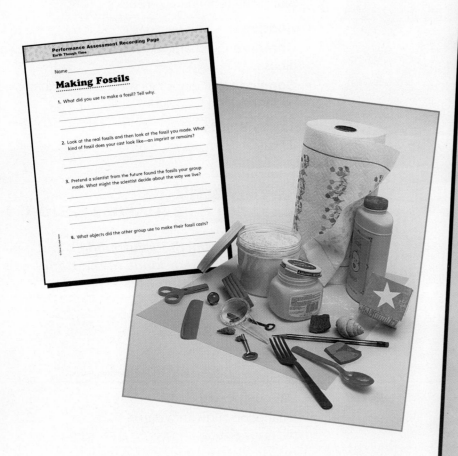

Children should have an understanding of the following science concepts by the end of the unit. These concepts are based upon the Benchmarks for Science Literacy produced by the American Association for the Advancement of Science (AAAS).

- Some kinds of organisms that once lived on earth have completely disappeared, although they were something like others that are alive today. (Lessons 1, 3, 4, 8, 9)

- A model of something is different from the real thing but can be used to learn something about the real thing. (Lessons 1, 4, 5, 6, 7)

- Simple graphs can help to tell about observations. (Lesson 2)

- Animals eat plants or other animals for food and may also use plants (or even other animals) for shelter and nesting. (Lesson 7)

Portfolio Assessment

Any product of a child's work, such as activity results, observations, experiment designs, and creative writing, related to this unit can be included in a child's portfolio. The Assessment Guide in the Teacher Resource Book provides instructions for having children choose and helping children evaluate portfolio selections.

Through the development and reinforcement of science process skills and critical thinking skills, **Scientific Reasoning Skills** are developed. The symbol shown here identifies questions within the teaching material that highlight Scientific Reasoning Skills.

LESSON 1

Investigating
CHARACTERISTICS OF DINOSAURS

In this **LESSON** children learn about characteristics of different kinds of dinosaurs.	In the **NEXT LESSON** children will learn that dinosaurs varied in size.

Resources

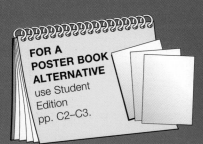

FOR A POSTER BOOK ALTERNATIVE use Student Edition pp. C2–C3.

POSTER BOOK p. C1 AND PICTURE CARDS C1, C2, C3, C4

ACTIVITY CARD C1

TRADE BOOK *How Big Were the Dinosaurs?*

Pacing Guide

Trade Book	15 minutes
Activity Card	20 minutes
Poster Book & Picture Cards	20 minutes

Teacher Resource Book
• *Home-School Connection*
• *Science Notebook*
• *Activity Support*
• *Assessment Guide*
• *Unit Project Pages*

 Videotape

  Audiotape or CD

 Equipment Kit

Lesson Overview

Science Themes: Models, Scale
Children examine dinosaur models. **Models** are scaled-down replicas. In these activities, children compare sizes and characteristics of dinosaur models prepared to **scale,** or a proportionally reduced size.

Project 2061 Benchmarks
• Some kinds of organisms that once lived on earth have completely disappeared, although they were something like others that are alive today.
• A model of something is different from the real thing but can be used to learn something about the real thing.

Concept
• Dinosaurs, which lived on land long ago, had many different characteristics.

Objectives
• **Compare** the characteristics of different types of dinosaurs.
• **Conclude** that dinosaurs were animals that lived on land a long time ago.

Science Words
dinosaur   model   reptile

Activity
Previewing
Activity Card C1

Children examine dinosaur models and generalize that different kinds of dinosaurs had similarities and differences.

Grouping
Small groups of 3–4

Materials
• Activity Card C1
• Dinosaur models*

Iguanodon (i gwan′ə dän)	30'
Pachycephalosaurus (pak ē sef ə lō sôr′es)	26'
Parasaurolophus (par ə sôr ə lō′fəs)	33'
Spinosaurus (spī nə sôr′əs)	39'
Triceratops (trī ser′ə täps)	30'
Tyrannosaurus (tə ran′ə sôr əs)	46'

• Hand lens*
• *Science Notebook* p. C17

**In Equipment Kit*

Pressed for Time?
This lesson targets a key concept in this unit. Use this lesson and Lessons 2, 3, 5, 6, and 9 if your teaching time is limited.

Science Background

Dinosaurs lived from 225 to 65 million years ago. The Mesozoic Era, or Age of Dinosaurs, is divided into three periods: Triassic (longest ago), Jurassic, and Cretaceous (most recent). By late Triassic times, dinosaurs were dominant. It was during this period that a single land mass, now called Pangaea broke apart into separate continents.

Some dinosaurs were probably cold-blooded and sluggish reptiles while others were more like warm-blooded mammals. Evidence has been found that they cared for their young, and many were active and fast-moving.

Real World Connection Scientists now think birds are descendants of dinosaurs.

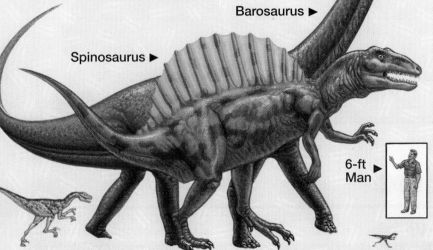

Barosaurus ▶

Spinosaurus ▶

6-ft Man ▶

▲ Deinonychus

Compsognathus ▲

Addressing Misconceptions

Cartoons such as "The Flintstones" may lead children to think that humans and dinosaurs lived at the same time. Point out that the last dinosaurs died about 65 million years before humans inhabited the earth.

Books for Children

Dinosaurs by Gail Gibbons (Holiday House, 1987). Introduces through simple text and illustrations the characteristics and habits of a variety of dinosaurs. (PreK–Grade 3)

My Visit to the Dinosaurs by Aliki (Harper Trophy, 1985). A visit to a museum of natural history provides a little boy with an introduction to the habits, characteristics, and habitats of 14 kinds of dinosaurs. (PreK–Grade 3)

The Trouble With Tyrannosaurus Rex by Lorinda Bryan Cauley. (Harcourt Brace Jovanovich, 1988). Ankylosaurus and Duckbill devise a plan with the other peaceful dinosaurs in their neighborhood to outwit and humiliate Tyrannosaurus Rex before he eats them all. (PreK–Grade 3)

Setting the Stage

Using the Trade Book

Read *How Big Were the Dinosaurs?* aloud. Explain that this book does not tell a story. It gives information about dinosaurs.

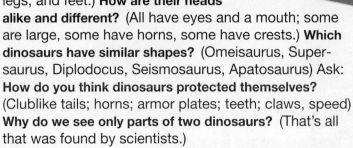

Display the drawings of dinosaurs at the back of the book. Ask: **How are these dinosaurs alike?** (They have heads, necks, tails, legs, and feet.) **How are their heads alike and different?** (All have eyes and a mouth; some are large, some have horns, some have crests.) **Which dinosaurs have similar shapes?** (Omeisaurus, Supersaurus, Diplodocus, Seismosaurus, Apatosaurus) Ask: **How do you think dinosaurs protected themselves?** (Clublike tails; horns; armor plates; teeth; claws, speed) **Why do we see only parts of two dinosaurs?** (That's all that was found by scientists.)

 **Assess Prior Knowledge**

Making a Baseline Assessment

Ask: **When did dinosaurs live? How did the earth look then? How did different dinosaurs look? What did different dinosaurs eat?** Record responses on chart paper and save them for comparison in Make a Final Assessment at the end of the lesson.

Using Technology

Audiotape or CD: *Grade 2 Science Songs*
After using Poster Book page C1, play the song "Dinosaur Tango" for the class. Have children listen to the words. Ask them if they would like to have a dinosaur for a pet and to explain why or why not.

Videotape: *Digging Up Dinosaurs*
Before beginning the lesson, show the videotape *Digging Up Dinosaurs* to the class. Have children discuss what they know about dinosaurs.

 Home-School Connection
As you begin the unit, distribute copies of the Unit Opening Letter (Teacher Resource Book page C3). Have children take the letters home to introduce the unit topic to their families.

Using the
ACTIVITY CARD

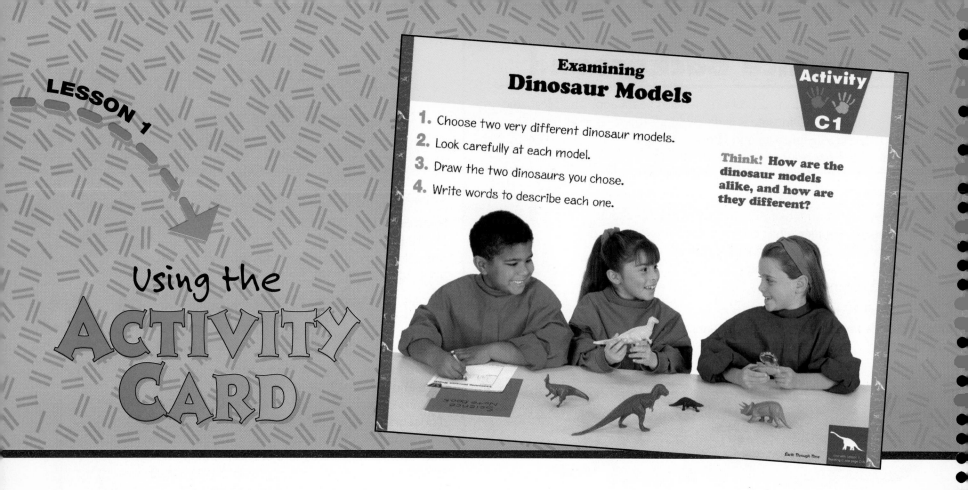

Examining
Dinosaur Models

Activity C1

1. Choose two very different dinosaur models.
2. Look carefully at each model.
3. Draw the two dinosaurs you chose.
4. Write words to describe each one.

Think! How are the dinosaur models alike, and how are they different?

Earth Through Time

Organize

Objective

- **Compare** the characteristics of different types of dinosaurs.

Process Skills

- **Use models** of dinosaurs to compare their sizes and shapes.
- **Observe** characteristics of dinosaurs as shown in models.

Pacing: 20 minutes

Grouping: Small groups of 3–4

Materials

- Activity Card C1
- Dinosaur models
- Hand lens
- *Science Notebook* p. C17

For Best Results: Demonstrate how to use a hand lens and discuss its importance as a scientific tool.

Guide

- **Warm-Up** Write the names of the dinosaur models on the chalkboard. Have children find identical syllables in the dinosaur names. Explain that *dino-* means terrible and *-saurus* means lizard. Although early scientists thought dinosaurs were lizards, we now know dinosaurs were not lizards.
- Help children visualize the sizes of the dinosaurs by measuring the length of the classroom and comparing each dinosaur with the classroom size.
- In step 1, direct each child to choose two dinosaur models to compare. Ask children to explain how the models resemble real dinosaurs.
- In step 2, have children compare the models using a hand lens to *observe* the special features of the dinosaurs they are examining.
- In step 3, have children *use the models* to outline the dinosaurs in their *Science Notebooks.* The drawings should approximate the dinosaurs' shapes.
- In step 4, help children to make a list of words describing the dinosaurs. Have them choose three words to write in their *Science Notebooks.*

👤 Responding To Individual Needs

Tactile/Kinesthetic Activity Measure the length of a child's step and have the child pace out the length of a dinosaur in the hallway. Ask children to name something else that might be that length.

 Expected Results

- Did children make accurate drawings of the sizes and shapes of the dinosaur models?
- Did children use the hand lens to examine the dinosaurs' body features closely?
- Did children's selection of descriptive words reveal that they noted what was different about their dinosaurs?

 Process Skills Checklist, Assessment Guide p. C68

Use the Process Skills Checklist to record children's performance.

- Did children *use* the *models* to compare the sizes and shapes of dinosaurs?
- Did children *observe* that different dinosaurs have different characteristics?

 Group Skills Checklist, Assessment Guide p. C69

Use the Group Skills Checklist to record children's performance.

- Did children *communicate clearly* the similarities and differences of the dinosaur models?
- Did they *listen* to each other's observations?

Close

- Ask: **Why did dinosaurs have different shapes and sizes?** (They adapted to their environment to get food and to protect themselves from other dinosaurs.)
- **Think!** Answer: Help children compare the sizes, body shapes, method of walking, and body features—tail, horns, crest, armor, teeth, spikes, claws.
- **Extend the Activity** Have children repeat the activity using different dinosaur models. Invite them to compare the results from the two sets of models. In the **multi-age classroom**, you may wish to have some children research the meanings of the names of dinosaurs and then share this information with the class.

 **Alternate Activity** TAKES LESS TIME

Pacing: 10 minutes
Grouping: Small groups of 3–4
Materials

- Dinosaur models
- Construction paper
- Lamp for projection of dinosaur image
- Crayons or colored pencils

Procedure

- Mount construction paper on a wall. Ask each group to choose a dinosaur model. Help each group in turn position the lamp and model so the shadow falls on a piece of construction paper. The shadow should be bigger than the model. Then have the group trace the outline of the dinosaur. Remind each group to write the name of their dinosaur and ask them to label any unique features.
- Discuss similarities and differences of the dinosaurs. Ask: **What are some features that all the dinosaurs have? What are some features that are different on different dinosaurs?** (All the dinosaurs have a head, neck, bodies, and four limbs. Features that differ include claws, armor plates, crests, spikes, size, weight, shape, and whether a dinosaur walks on four legs or two.) You may wish to use copies of the Activity Support blackline master titled "Venn Diagram" (Teacher Resource Book page C35) when comparing the features of the dinosaurs.

Using the POSTER BOOK & PICTURE CARDS

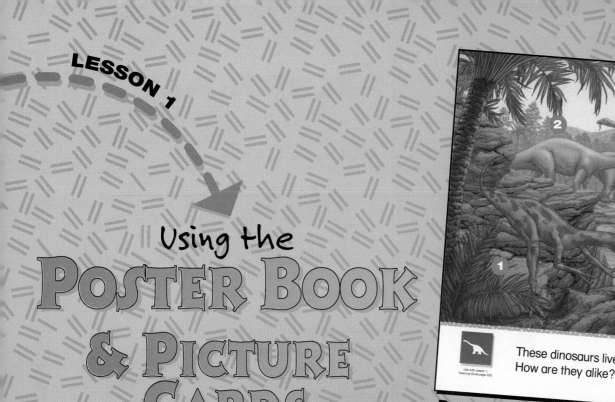

These dinosaurs lived on the earth a long time ago. How are they alike? How are they different?

Use with Lesson 1, Teaching Guide page C20

Earth Through Time C1

POSTER BOOK PAGE

① Ornitholestes (ôr′ni thə les′tēz) 6½' ② Diplodocus (di pläd′ə kəs) 88' ③ Brachiosaurus (brak′ē ə sôr əs) 75'
④ Allosaurus (al ō sôr′əs) 39'

Organize

Objectives

- **Compare** the characteristics of different types of dinosaurs.
- **Conclude** that dinosaurs were animals that lived on land a long time ago.

Process Skill

- **Observe** that different kinds of dinosaurs had different characteristics.

Pacing: 20 minutes

Grouping: Whole class

Materials
- Poster Book p. C1
- Picture Cards C1, C2, C3, C4
  (See backs of Picture Cards for questions, facts, and related activities.)
- Erasable marker

For Best Results: If you use an erasable marker on the Poster Book page, wipe it off immediately after the lesson.

Using the Student Edition: You may wish to use Student Edition pages C2–C3 to extend or replace the Poster Book lesson.

Guide

- **Warm-Up** Remind children there were many different kinds of dinosaurs. Be sure children understand the vocabulary words **dinosaur** (now-extinct animal of the Mesozoic Era), **model** (miniature replica), and **reptile** (cold-blooded and scaly-skinned animal that lays eggs).
- **Poster Book** Display Poster Book page C1. Ask: **How many different kinds of dinosaurs are in the picture?** (Four) Have children use an erasable marker to write a number by each different kind of dinosaur. Write the numbers and the names of the dinosaurs below the picture. Help children pronounce the names.
- Ask: **What is alike and what is different about these dinosaurs?** (All have four limbs, a head, and a tail. Diplodocus and Brachiosaurus are larger, have long necks, walk on four stumpy legs, and are plant eaters. Ornitholestes and Allosaurus have sharp pointed teeth, walk on two legs, and are meat eaters.) *(observe)* Help children conclude from the setting that the dinosaurs lived on land. Ask: **What was the land and climate like when dinosaurs lived on the earth?** (Many big trees and plants; warm, many active volcanoes)
- **Picture Cards** Have children compare the characteristics of Apatosaurus (a dinosaur), Velociraptor (a dinosaur), Elasmosaurus (a sea reptile), and Pteranodon (a flying reptile). Point out that Elasmosaurus and Pteranodon were not dinosaurs. Dinosaurs were reptiles that lived on land and did not fly.

👤 Responding To Individual Needs

Inclusive Activity   Have children use an erasable marker to draw a circle around the parts of the dinosaurs on the Poster Book that are different and draw a square around the parts that are similar. Ask them to name the parts that are different and the parts that are similar.

C1: Apatosaurus
C2: Velociraptor
C3: Elasmosaurus
C4: Pteranodon

Close

 Explain that dinosaurs, as well as many other species, became extinct about 65 million years ago, but scientists aren't sure why. The earth may have become much colder, and the dinosaurs could not live in the cold weather. Ask: **How are animals today able to live where they do?** (Children might discuss how polar bears, giraffes, whales, and other animals are suited to their environment.)

 Extend the Activity Have children draw a picture of how they think the earth might look 65 million years in the future. Ask: **Do you think animals will be the same sizes and shapes as they are now in 65 million years? Why?** (Children may respond that animals will be different because the weather and available food may be different in the future.)

Assess
CONCEPT DEVELOPMENT

 Concept Checklist, Assessment Guide p. C71

Use the Concept Checklist to record children's understanding.

- Do children recognize that dinosaurs have some characteristics in common and some that are different?
- Do children realize that dinosaurs lived on land along with other kinds of animals?

 Lesson Assessment, Assessment Guide p. C48

Use the Lesson 1 Assessment to evaluate children's understanding of the lesson concept.

 Discussion Starters

Ask questions like the following to stimulate class discussion:

- **What animals today have any features that are like the dinosaurs'?** (Elephant's legs, bull's horns, and giraffe's neck)
- **How do today's animals use these parts?** (Walking, defense, and reaching food)

Drawing

Invite children to imagine and draw their own dinosaurs and decide where their dinosaurs would live, what they would eat, and how they would protect themselves.

 ## Science & Language Arts

DESCRIBING DINOSAURS Invite children to describe their favorite dinosaurs to the class, including their sizes, what they ate, and how they moved. If possible, have children display drawings of the dinosaurs and explain why those dinosaurs are favorites. You may wish to have children use copies of the Activity Support blackline master titled "Chart/Survey" (Teacher Resource Book page C34) to record their descriptions.

 ## Science & Math

MEASURING LENGTH Help children mark the hallway with masking tape every ten feet. Display the dinosaur models. Have children mark the actual length of the dinosaurs and compare the sizes. Suggest that children also compare sizes to something familiar, such as the length of the playground. Help children discover that by labeling 10' as 1, 20' as 2, and 30' as 3, they can determine which dinosaurs are two or three times as long as others.

INVESTIGATE FURTHER

UNIT PROJECT LINK

Dinosaur Place: Making a Dinosaur Chart

Discuss with children the idea of making a Dinosaur Place exhibit in the classroom. On the Unit Project page have them list their favorite dinosaurs and each dinosaur's characteristics, such as size, shape of head, number of legs, and type of food eaten.

Then help children make a large Dinosaur Chart. The chart should have spaces for dinosaurs' names across the top and spaces for characteristics under the name of each dinosaur. Have children choose which dinosaurs they want to include in the exhibit and then fill in the spaces on the chart. Hang the chart in the classroom as a centerpiece for their Dinosaur Place exhibit.

Use Unit Project page C97 in the Teacher Resource Book with this activity.

In the Science Center

Learning More About Dinosaurs

Objective
- **Compare** the characteristics of different types of dinosaurs.

Process Skill
- **Infer** that each dinosaur was equipped to do some things better than other things.

Pacing: 10 minutes

Grouping: Pairs

Materials
- Dinosaur models
- Picture Cards C1 and C2

Procedure
- Ask each child to choose one of the dinosaur models or Picture Card C1 or C2 and describe the dinosaur's size and body features to a partner.

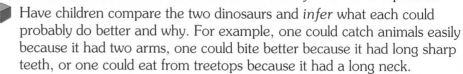 Have children compare the two dinosaurs and *infer* what each could probably do better and why. For example, one could catch animals easily because it had two arms, one could bite better because it had long sharp teeth, or one could eat from treetops because it had a long neck.

Make a FINAL ASSESSMENT

 Review the *Science Notebook*

Ask questions to find out whether children remember and understand the concept that different kinds of dinosaurs had different characteristics.

 Return to Baseline Assessment

Display children's responses to the Assess Prior Knowledge questions. Read the responses aloud. Ask children if they want to make changes or add information to the chart.

 Group Discussion

On the chalkboard, draw a chart with the names of several dinosaurs listed in the left column. Write the column heads *length, head and neck, legs, feet and toes* across the top. Invite children to examine the dinosaur models and Picture Cards and contribute appropriate words to write in each column.

 Writing

Have children contribute to a chart story about going back to the time of the dinosaurs. Ask questions to help children suggest sentences describing what the earth was like then.

Have children save their work for the portfolio selection process at the end of the unit.

Home-School Connection

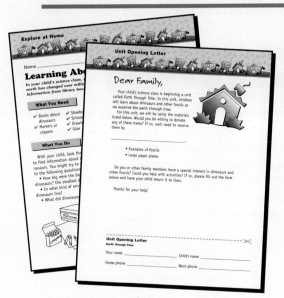

The Family Letter that begins this unit (Teacher Resource Book page C3) introduces the topic of the earth through time. The Explore at Home activity "Learning About Dinosaurs" (Teacher Resource Book page C4) invites children to make a dinosaur diorama. After children have done the activity with their families and have brought in their dioramas, have children share their dioramas with the class.

Science & Math

COUNTING YEARS Help children develop their concepts of time by placing 10 equal-sized pieces of crayon next to each other to represent 10 years. Measure the crayons with a ruler. Have children measure the length 10 times to show 100 years. Ask them to show 1,000 years. Then explain that one million years is 1,000 times 1,000. Dinosaurs lived on the earth from 225 million years ago to 65 million years ago.

Looking Ahead

Now that the children have learned that different dinosaurs had different characteristics, they will learn that dinosaurs varied in size.

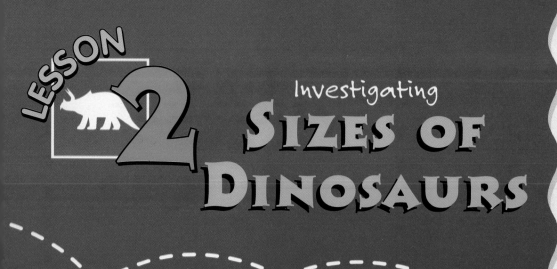

LESSON 2

Investigating SIZES OF DINOSAURS

In the **LAST LESSON** children learned about characteristics of different kinds of dinosaurs.

In this **LESSON** children learn that dinosaurs varied in size.

In the **NEXT LESSON** children will learn that fossils show how ancient plants and animals looked.

Resources

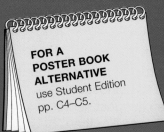

FOR A POSTER BOOK ALTERNATIVE use Student Edition pp. C4–C5.

POSTER BOOK p. C2

ACTIVITY CARD C2

TRADE BOOK *How Big Were the Dinosaurs?*

Pacing Guide

Trade Book	15 minutes
Activity Card	20 minutes
Poster Book	20 minutes

Teacher Resource Book
• *Home-School Connection*
• *Science Notebook*
• *Activity Support*
• *Assessment Guide*
• *Unit Project Pages*

Audiotape or CD

Equipment Kit

Lesson Overview

Science Theme: Scale
Children compare pictures of dinosaurs. In these activities, they observe dinosaurs drawn to **scale**, a proportionally reduced size. They use the scale to calculate the sizes of dinosaurs relative to their own sizes or the sizes of familiar objects.

Project 2061 Benchmark
• Simple graphs can help to tell about observations.

Concept
• Fossils provide evidence that some dinosaurs were among the largest animals that have ever lived and that others were quite small.

Objectives
• **Compare** the sizes of dinosaurs to a child's size.
• **Compare** the sizes of dinosaurs to other objects that the children estimate to be the same size as the dinosaurs.

Science Words
Compsognathus (cämp säg'nə thəs) 2½'
Lambeosaurus (lam bē ō sôr'əs) 50'
Stegosaurus (steg ə sôr'əs) 30'
Styracosaurus (stī räk' ō sôr'əs) 18'
Triceratops (tri ser'ə täps) 30'
Velociraptor (və läs'ə rap tər) 6'

 Previewing **Activity Card C2**

Children observe drawings of dinosaurs projected to actual size on a wall. They measure the projected drawings and observe that the dinosaurs were different sizes.

Grouping
Whole class

Materials
• Activity Card C2   • Yardstick
• Activity Support blackline masters: Stegosaurus, Compsognathus, Styracosaurus
• Overhead projector
• *Science Notebook* p. C18

Advance Preparation
Use acetate and a copy machine to make transparencies from the blackline masters. Arrange to use the gymnasium and a projector.

* *In Equipment Kit*

 Pressed for Time?
This lesson targets a key concept in this unit. Use this lesson and Lessons 1, 3, 5, 6, and 9 if your teaching time is limited.

Science Background

When scientists find dinosaur bones, they begin by making a grid or diagram showing the location of each bone. Bones are often jumbled when they are found. Identifying the bones and placing them in their proper positions is like completing a jigsaw puzzle. Next, casts are made of actual bones. Missing bones are sculpted based on scientists' knowledge of other dinosaurs. Then models may be mounted in lifelike poses.

Real World Connection Children may be able to view models of dinosaurs in museums.

Addressing
Misconceptions

Because of cartoons and motion pictures, children may believe that all dinosaurs were much bigger than humans. Explain that some dinosaurs were small, as are many animals that we see today.

Books for Children

The Dinosaur Data Book: The Definitive, Fully Illustrated Encyclopedia of Dinosaurs **by David Lambert and Diagram Visual Information Ltd. (Avon Books, 1990).** Provides information on various dinosaurs. Information may be read aloud and the illustrations shared to enhance children's understanding of lesson concepts. (Grades 3–8)

Dinosaurium **by Barbara Brenner (Bantam Books, 1993).** Describes a museum tour through the Triassic, Jurassic, and Cretaceous Periods, with information about the names and habitats of the dinosaurs. Includes questions for the reader to answer. (PreK–Grade 3)

The Rourke Dinosaur Dictionary **by Joseph Hincks (Rourke Enterprises, Inc., 1988).** Describes the physical characteristics and habits of dinosaurs. It has an alphabet arrangement. Use with your advanced or motivated students. (Grade K and up)

Setting the
Stage

Using the Trade Book

Reread aloud parts of *How Big Were the Dinosaurs?* in which the author compares dinosaur sizes. Display pages showing Stegosaurus and Triceratops.

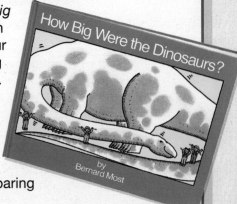

Ask: **What is wrong with these pictures?** (There were no houses, children, or cars when dinosaurs lived.) **Why are these objects in the picture?** (To show sizes by comparing dinosaurs to familiar things)

Ask: **How can we find out exactly how big something is?** (Measure the actual size with a ruler, yardstick, or other measure.) Help children conclude that photos and models show how something looks and the relative size of things, but don't show actual sizes.

Activity — Assess Prior Knowledge

Making a Baseline Assessment
Ask: **Were dinosaurs bigger or smaller than you are? Were all dinosaurs the same size? How long do you think the biggest dinosaur was? How do we know how big different dinosaurs were?** Record responses on chart paper and save them for comparison in Make a Final Assessment at the end of the lesson.

Using Technology

Audiotape or CD: *Grade 2 Science Songs*
After using Activity Card C2, play the song "Dinosaur Tango" for the class. Have children pretend they are dinosaurs and do a dinosaur dance.

Using the
ACTIVITY CARD

Comparing
Sizes of Dinosaurs

Activity **C2**

1. Stand next to the dinosaur picture on the wall and compare the size of the dinosaur to your size.

2. Measure the length of the dinosaur. Record the length.

3. Repeat steps 1 and 2 for each dinosaur picture.

4. Make a bar graph to compare the lengths of the dinosaurs.

Think! Which dinosaurs were bigger than you?

3 feet

Earth Through Time

Organize

Objective

- **Compare** the sizes of dinosaurs to a child's size.

Process Skills

- **Measure** the sizes of dinosaurs.
- **Collect, record,** and **interpret data** about the sizes of dinosaurs.

Pacing: 20 minutes

Grouping: Whole class

Materials

- Activity Card C2
- Dinosaur pictures
- Yardstick
- *Science Notebook* p. C18

Guide

- **Warm-Up** Place a transparency on the projector stage and turn on the projector. Move the projector away from the wall until the I-bar is 3 feet wide. Hold up a yardstick and explain to children that the length of a yardstick is 1 yard—which equals 3 feet. Show children the I-bar on the unprojected transparency. Explain that the little I-bar length represents the length of the yardstick. Ask: **What will we see if we make the I-bar the length of a yardstick?** (How big the dinosaur really was)

- In step 1, as a child stands next to the projected dinosaur, have children compare the dinosaur's size to the child's size.

- In step 2, have one child use the yardstick to *measure* the length of each projected dinosaur **(Stegosaurus, Compsognathus,** and **Styracosaurus).** Invite other children to point on the dinosaur where the yardstick ends so children can count the number of yardstick lengths needed to measure the dinosaur. Help children to count each yardstick length as 3 feet and to record the lengths of each dinosaur in their *Science Notebook. (collect* and *record data)*

- Before children do step 4, be sure they understand what a bar graph is. Children may wish to turn the *Science Notebook* page sideways so the lines go the same direction as the length of the dinosaur. Have children color in the bar graph.

Responding To Individual Needs

Inclusive Activity   After children measure the three dinosaurs, have them write the lengths on the chalkboard or on a large piece of paper. Then ask children to compare the sizes of the dinosaurs. Encourage them to rank the dinosaurs from largest to smallest by saying or writing numbers 1, 2, 3 for each dinosaur.

 Expected Results

- Did children use the yardstick to measure the lengths of the dinosaurs?
- Did children record the dinosaurs' lengths accurately, using the scale on the graph?

 Process Skills Checklist
Assessment Guide p. C68

Use the Process Skills Checklist to record children's performance.

- Did children accurately *measure* the actual sizes of the dinosaurs?
- Did children *collect, record,* and *interpret data* about the sizes of dinosaurs?

 Group Skills Checklist
Assessment Guide p. C69

Use the Group Skills Checklist to record children's performance.

- Did children *take initiative* to participate in measuring the dinosaurs?
- Did they *communicate clearly* their impressions of the sizes of the dinosaurs?
- Did they *listen* to each other's observations?

Close

 Ask: **How big were dinosaurs?** (Children may suggest that dinosaurs were different sizes. Some were very big.) *(interpret data)*

- **Think!** Answer: Stegosaurus and Styracosaurus were bigger than people.
- **Extend the Activity** Have children make verbal size comparisons of the dinosaurs to objects in the world today. Help them think of living and nonliving things for comparison. In the **multi-age classroom**, you may wish to have some children make another bar graph comparing the lengths of other dinosaurs.

 **TAKES LESS TIME**

Pacing: 10 minutes
Grouping: Individual
Advance Preparation

Duplicate enough copies of Activity Support blackline masters Stegosaurus, Compsognathus, and Styracosaurus to give one to each child.

Materials

- Copies of Activity Support blackline masters titled Stegosaurus, Compsognathus, Styracosaurus
- Scissors
- Yardstick
- *Science Notebook* p. C18

Procedure

- Have children carefully cut out the I-bar scale on the blackline master. Help them use it to measure each dinosaur, marking where the scale ends each time they move it. Write the number of lengths above each mark, for example, 1, 2, 3. Explain that the scale represents 3 feet. Help children to record each dinosaur's length in *feet* on the bar graph on the *Science Notebook* page.
- Move to the hallway. Beginning at the same place each time, have children use a yardstick to measure the actual lengths of the dinosaurs.
- Then measure a child with a yardstick to compare the dinosaurs' sizes to the child's size.

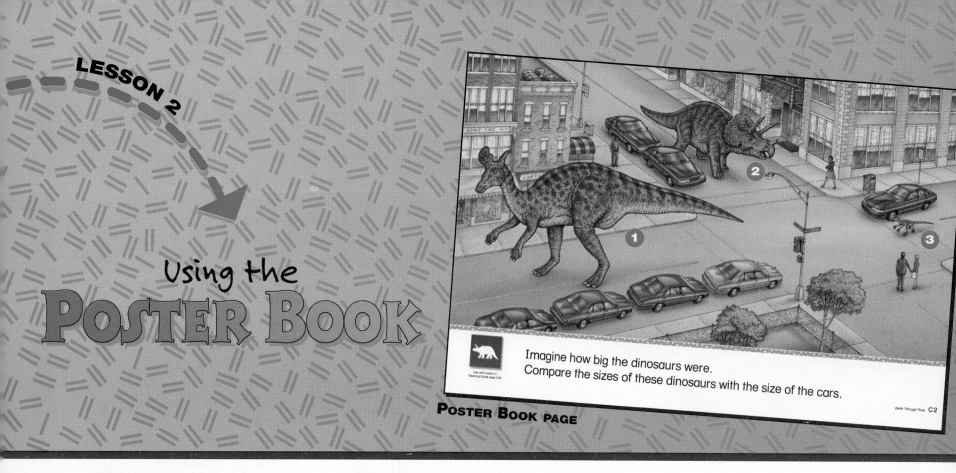

LESSON 2

Using the
POSTER BOOK

Imagine how big the dinosaurs were.
Compare the sizes of these dinosaurs with the size of the cars.

POSTER BOOK PAGE

Earth Through Time C2

➊ **Lambeosaurus** (lam bē ō sôr′əs) ➋ **Triceratops** (trī ser′ə täps) ➌ **Velociraptor** (və läs′ə rap tər)

Organize

Objective

- **Compare** the sizes of dinosaurs to other objects that the children estimate to be the same size as the dinosaurs.

Process Skills

- **Observe** three kinds of dinosaurs.
- **Measure** the lengths and heights of the dinosaurs.

Pacing: 20 minutes

Grouping: Whole class

Materials

- Poster Book p. C2
- Erasable marker
- Scissors
- Several sheets of paper

Using the Student Edition: You may wish to use Student Edition pages C4–C5 to extend or replace the Poster Book lesson.

Guide

- **Warm-Up** Remind children that dinosaurs were many different sizes and did not live at the same time as humans. Ask: **What are some of the tallest objects in your neighborhood?** (Children might say trees, buildings, telephone wires, hills, a water tower, or the school itself.) **Were there dinosaurs larger and smaller than these neighborhood objects?** (Probably larger than many of the objects, but some were smaller, and there might be a tower taller or a mountain larger than a dinosaur)
- **Poster Book** Have children find the three dinosaurs on the Poster Book page. *(observe)* Ask them if they can name the dinosaurs. (Some children might be familiar with the **Triceratops**, and maybe with the **Velociraptor** and the **Lambeosaurus**.) Ask them to point to the largest dinosaur. (Lambeosaurus) Ask: **Which is the smallest dinosaur?** (Velociraptor)
- Discuss with children the difference in the sizes of the dinosaurs. Let them compare the dinosaurs to their surroundings, and predict if any of the objects are about the same size of the dinosaurs.

  Help children cut a strip of paper the length of one of the cars on the Poster Book page. Tell them they will use the paper to *measure* the length of each dinosaur. Each car in the picture is about 15 feet long. Ask: **How many cars long is each dinosaur?** (Lambeosaurus: about 3⅓ car lengths long, Triceratops: about 2 car lengths long, Velociraptor: about ½ car length long)

Responding To Individual Needs

Children Acquiring English Proficiency   Have children use the numbers in their native language and in English to estimate the length of the dinosaurs. For children used to the metric system, explain that a yard is a little shorter than a meter.

CONCEPT DEVELOPMENT

 Concept Checklist, Assessment Guide p. C72

Use the Concept Checklist to record children's understanding of the lesson concept.

- Do children recognize that dinosaurs were a wide variety of sizes?
- Do children understand that some dinosaurs were much larger than humans, and some were smaller?

 Lesson Assessment, Assessment Guide p. C49

Use the Lesson 2 Assessment to evaluate children's understanding of the lesson concept.

 Interview

Have children describe for a radio audience their favorite dinosaur. Encourage children to compare the dinosaur's size and shape with their own size and shape and the size and shape of other objects. Let them use their imagination to describe how they felt when they met the dinosaur.

 Debate

Debate the topic: The scariest dinosaur we studied is *(name)*. Have children use the sentence format: The dinosaur's *(name/body part)* is as big as *(object or other living animal)*. Vary the initial topic with the words *cutest, strangest,* or other words that the children suggest.

Close

■ Discuss the overall sizes of the dinosaurs as well as the sizes of their specific body parts. Ask: **How do the dinosaurs compare in size with the objects in the poster?** Have children respond with sentences using *much smaller, smaller, as big as, bigger than,* and *much bigger than.*

■ **Extend the Activity** Ask: **What are some objects that are about the same lengths as these dinosaurs?** (Children may compare dinosaurs with objects or rooms in the school or equipment on the playground.) In the **multi-age classroom**, you may wish to have some children measure the actual lengths of the objects used for comparison.

 ## Science & Social Studies

USING A SCALE Have children explain how they used the I-bar scale to measure the sizes of the dinosaurs and why people need to use scales. Then have them find the scale on a map and use the scale to measure the sizes of some countries. As an alternative, have them use the size of their state as a scale and locate other states that are just as wide, half as wide, or twice as wide.

 ## Science & Math

MAKING A GRAPH Have children make a bar graph, using copies of Activity Support blackline master titled "2-cm Grid" (Teacher Resource Book page C31). The graph should show how many car lengths long the Lambeosaurus, Triceratops, and Velociraptor on Poster Book page C2 are. Tell children that each car length is about 15 feet. Help children conclude that using a graph helps us compare objects. We can compare the lengths to the size of something we know.

INVESTIGATE FURTHER

UNIT PROJECT LINK

Dinosaur Place: Drawing Dinosaurs

Have each child select a dinosaur listed on the Dinosaur Chart and draw it on the Unit Project page. Then have them color their dinosaur, mount it on construction paper or tagboard, and cut it out. Encourage children as they make their drawings to keep in mind the relative sizes of dinosaurs.

Help children mount the cut-out drawings around the room, using string and masking tape. Children may work on this activity throughout the unit.

Use Unit Project page C98 in the Teacher Resource Book with this activity.

In the Science Center

Learning More About Dinosaurs

Objective
- **Compare** the sizes of dinosaurs to a child's size.

Process Skills
- **Observe** the relative sizes of dinosaurs.

Pacing: 10 minutes

Grouping: Pairs

Materials
- Crayons or colored pencils   • Scissors
- Duplicates of Activity Support blackline masters: Stegosaurus, Compsognathus, Styracosaurus, 2-cm Grid
- *Science Notebook* p. C18

Procedure
- Display copies of Activity Support blackline masters titled "Stegosaurus," "Compsognathus," and "Styracosaurus" (Teacher Resource Book pages C36, C37, and C38). Have children review the bar graphs they made in their Science Notebooks for Activity Card C2 and compare the sizes of the dinosaurs (30', 18', 2½'). *(observe)*
- Invite children to draw pictures of the three dinosaurs and a favorite living animal, using copies of Activity Support blackline master titled "2-cm Grid" (Teacher Resource Book page C31). Tell children to assume that each square equals 3 feet. When children have completed their drawings, they should cut them out and compare the sizes.

Make a
FINAL ASSESSMENT

✓ Review the *Science Notebook*

Ask questions to see if children understand that some dinosaurs were the biggest land animals that ever lived, while others were quite small.

✓ Return to Baseline Assessment

Display children's responses to the Assess Prior Knowledge questions. Read them aloud and have children make changes and add information learned in the lesson.

✓ Designing

Help children collect measurements of dinosaurs' heights and lengths, using the Activity Card information and any classroom or available library resources. When there are measurements for 10 dinosaurs or more, help children design a graph on poster board showing the variety of sizes of dinosaurs. They can use small pictures or drawings of the dinosaurs to paste on the graph, marking lengths and heights. Then add their own pictures (copies from class pictures) or pictures of objects for comparison. You may wish to have children use copies of the Activity Support blackline masters titled "Chart/Survey" (Teacher Resource Book page C34) and "2-cm Grid" (Teacher Resource Book page C31) to record data and design a graph.

Have children save their work for the portfolio selection process at the end of the unit.

Home-School Connection

The Explore at Home activity "Bigger Than a Breadbox" (Teacher Resource Book page C5) invites children to look through books about dinosaurs and then draw a picture that shows the child's own height compared with the height or length of a dinosaur. After children have done the activity with their families and have brought in their drawings, invite children to share them with the class.

 ## Science & Math

COMPARING ANIMALS Have children compare the sizes of the dinosaurs with the sizes of animals living today. Discuss where the larger animals live today and how their habitats compare with the setting shown on Poster Book page C2. Invite children to use copies of the Activity Support blackline master titled "Word Web" (Teacher Resource Book, p. C32) to make comparisons of animals and habitats.

 ## Looking Ahead

Now that children have learned that dinosaurs varied in size, they will learn that fossils show how early plants and animals looked.

LESSON 3

Investigating KINDS OF FOSSILS

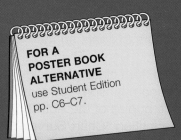

In the **LAST LESSON** children learned that dinosaurs varied in size.

In this **LESSON** children learn that fossils show how earlier plants and animals looked.

In the **NEXT LESSON** children will learn how fossil imprints are made.

Resources

POSTER BOOK p. C3

FOR A POSTER BOOK ALTERNATIVE use Student Edition pp. C6–C7.

ACTIVITY CARD C3

TRADE BOOK
Fossils Tell of Long Ago

Pacing Guide	
Trade Book	15 minutes
Activity Card	20 minutes
Poster Book	20 minutes

Teacher Resource Book
• *Home-School Connection*
• *Science Notebook*
• *Activity Support*
• *Assessment Guide*
• *Unit Project Pages*

Equipment Kit

Lesson Overview

Science Theme: Models
Children examine fossil imprints and fossil remains. These fossils can be used as **models** to learn what early plants and animals looked like. Both imprints and remains are actual-size models rather than scale models.

Project 2061 Benchmark
• Some kinds of organisms that once lived on earth have completely disappeared, although they were something like others that are alive today.

Concept
• Some fossils are the remains of once-living things; some fossils are the imprints of once-living things.

Objective
• **Compare** fossil imprints with fossil remains.

Science Words
fossils
imprints
remains

Activity — Previewing Activity Card C3

Children examine fossils and generalize that fossils tell us about the sizes, shapes, and appearance of plants and animals that lived long ago.

Grouping
Small groups of 3–4

Materials
• Activity Card C3
• Fossil imprint of a fern*
• Fossil remains of a snail*
• Hand lens*
• *Science Notebook* p. C19

For Best Results
Explain to children that they should handle the fossils as carefully as scientists do because the fossils cannot be replaced if they are damaged. Review use of the hand lens.

*In Equipment Kit

 Pressed for Time?
This lesson targets a key concept in this unit. Use this lesson and Lessons 1, 2, 5, 6, and 9 if your teaching time is limited.

Science Background

Fossils, or preserved evidence of earlier life, exist in many forms. The earliest animals, with no hard shells, left evidence of their trails, or imprints of their bodies. In later fossils, actual bone, skin, shell, leaves, twigs, nuts, or spores may still remain. Hard parts may be replaced in varying amounts by silicon, calcium, carbon, or minerals such as pyrite. Some shells or bones buried in mud may be partially or completely replaced. Some shells dissolve and the empty space is filled with other material to form casts and molds. Imprints and footprints are other kinds of fossils.

Real World Connection Explain that people still search for and find fossils. Look for articles on fossil finds in newspapers and magazines.

Addressing
Misconceptions

Children may believe that all plants and animals become fossils, but the conditions necessary for preservation are very rare. Explain that when most plants and animals die, they break down into their component chemicals, which go into the soil.

Books for Children

Digging Up Dinosaurs by Aliki (Harper & Row, 1988, 1981). Easy-reader format briefly introduces various types of dinosaurs whose skeletons and reconstructions are seen in museums and explains how scientists uncover, preserve, and study fossilized dinosaur bones. (PreK–Grade 3)

Fossils by Allan Roberts (Childrens Press, 1983). Explains how the remains of an animal or plant fossilize over millions of years, where fossils may be found, and what we can learn from them. (Grades K–4)

Janice VanCleave's Dinosaurs for Every Kid: Easy Activities That Make Science Fun by Janice VanCleave (John Wiley, 1994). Contains activities that provide insights into the concepts presented in the unit and lesson and may be used in the Science Center to further enhance children's understanding. (Grades 2–5)

Setting the
Stage

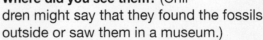

Using the Trade Book

Read aloud *Fossils Tell of Long Ago.* Ask: **Where does the story say you might find fossils?** (At the seashore, in the woods, in the mountains, in limestone.) **What kinds of fossils have you seen?** (Children might describe imprints in rocks or fossilized bones.) **Where did you see them?** (Children might say that they found the fossils outside or saw them in a museum.)

Why is the fish in the story called a fossil? (It lived a long time ago and an impression of its body was preserved.) **How did the fish in the story become a fossil?** (Mud covered it and turned to rock. Only its bones, or minerals in the bones, are left.) **What things become fossils?** (Many animals and plants become fossils.) ■ **How do fossils tell about life long ago?** (They show how plants and animals looked in early times.) **Is a dead fish on the beach a fossil? Why not?** (It's too recent; it's not preserved.) **What will happen to the fish if it stays on the beach?** (The body will decompose or break down, leaving only bones.) **What will happen to the bones?** (They'll be washed away, eaten or broken, or slowly decay or rot.)

 **Assess Prior Knowledge**

Making a Baseline Assessment
Ask: **What is a fossil? Do all plants and animals become fossils when they die? What can fossils tell us about life on earth long, long ago? Are there any fossils of life on the earth today?** Record responses on chart paper and save them for comparison in Make a Final Assessment at the end of the lesson.

Using the ACTIVITY CARD

Examining Fossils

Activity C3

1. Look closely at two fossils. Record what you see.

2. Discuss what kinds of living things made these fossils. Decide if they were plants or animals when they were alive.

3. Draw how you think these plants or animals looked.

Think! How are the two fossils alike, and how are they different?

Organize

Objective

- **Compare** fossil imprints with fossil remains.

Process Skills

- **Communicate** the characteristics of fossil imprints and fossil remains.
- **Collect, record,** and **interpret data** describing each fossil.

Pacing: 20 minutes

Grouping: Small groups of 3–4

Materials

- Activity Card C3
- 2 fossils
- Hand lens
- *Science Notebook* p. C19

Guide

- **Warm-Up** Ask why the children on the Activity Card are using a hand lens. Help children conclude that fossils are very, very old and they must look carefully to make sure they see all the details.
- Have children compare the **fossils** in step 1 and describe what they see. *(collect data, communicate)* Explain that fossils are traces of once-living things. One of the fossils is an **imprint,** which shows what is left when a plant or animal is pressed against something, a process that works like a rubber stamp. The other fossil is the **remains** of a plant or animal. It is a part of that plant or animal.
- Have children write words on *Science Notebook* page C19 that tell *(communicate* and *record data)* exactly what each fossil looks like so that someone could picture it by reading the words.
- In step 2, have children suggest modern living things that look like each fossil to help them decide whether the fossils are plant or animal.
- In step 3, have children draw in their *Science Notebooks* how they think the plant or animal looked when it was alive. *(interpret data)*

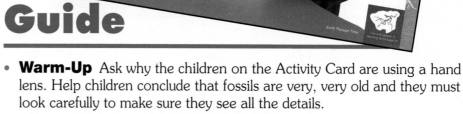

Responding To Individual Needs

<u>Tactile/Kinesthetic Activity</u>   Have children place a sheet of paper over the imprint and, pressing down lightly, use a crayon or pencil to color over the imprint until its shape appears. Ask them to describe the shape and texture of the rubbing.

 Expected Results

- Did children handle the fossils carefully and use the hand lens properly to look for details of the fossils?
- Did their drawings resemble what the plant and animal might have looked like?
- Did children collect, record, and interpret the data correctly?

 Process Skills Checklist
Assessment Guide p. C68

Use the Process Skills Checklist to record children's performance.

- Did children choose appropriate words to *communicate* what the plant and animal fossils looked like?
- Did children *collect, record,* and *interpret* the *data* correctly?

 Group Skills Checklist
Assessment Guide p. C69

Use the Group Skills Checklist to record children's performance.

- Did children *encourage* each other to participate in the activity?
- Did they *discuss* what kinds of living things they believed had made the fossils?

Close

- Discuss with children why they might like to find a fossil. (Children may suggest that fossils are hard to find and it would be fun to figure out how the plant or animal looked.)
- **Think!** Answer: Both are traces of once-living things. One is the imprint of a plant and the other is the remains of an animal.
- **Extend the Activity** Invite children to bring pictures of fossils or real fossils from home. In class, have them copy or cut out pictures of fossils from magazines so that each child has at least one "fossil." Ask children to put imprint fossils on one table and fossil remains on another table. As they put the fossils down, ask them to explain why they are imprints or remains.

 Alternate **Activity** TAKES LESS TIME

Pacing: 10 minutes
Grouping: Individual
Materials
- Overhead projector
- Fossil imprint of a leaf
- Fossil remains of a snail

Procedure
- Project enlarged fossils, one at a time, on the wall or a white chalkboard.

- Have children observe the markings from the fossils and draw them.
- Discuss the appearance of each fossil. Then have children draw how they think the plant or animal looked when it was alive.
- Conclude with the children's comparison of how the two fossils are alike and different. You may wish to have children use copies of the Activity Support blackline master titled "Venn Diagram" (Teacher Resource Book page C35) to compare the two fossils.

INVESTIGATING KINDS OF FOSSILS **C35**

LESSON 3

Using the
POSTER BOOK

Find the fossil remains. Find the fossil imprints.
Why are fossils important to scientists?

POSTER BOOK PAGE

Earth Through Time C3

➊ Fossil remains and imprints of shells
➌ Fossil imprint of fern

➋ Fossil imprint of fish
➍ Mammoth fossils at Hot Springs

Organize

Objective

• **Compare** fossil imprints with fossil remains.

Process Skill

• **Infer** whether a fossil is an imprint or remains and what plant or animal today looks like the fossil.

Pacing: 20 minutes

Grouping: Whole class

Materials
• Poster Book p. C3
• Erasable markers

For Best Results: If you use an erasable marker on the Poster Book page, wipe it off immediately after the lesson.

Using the Student Edition: You may wish to use Student Edition pages C6–C7 to extend or replace the Poster Book lesson.

Guide

• **Warm-Up** Remind children that imprint fossils show what is left when a plant or animal was pressed against mud, rock, or another substance that later hardened. Fossil remains are actual parts of a plant or animal, which may be entirely or partially replaced by minerals.

• **Poster Book** Display Poster Book page C3. Have children compare the fossils pictured on this page and *infer* which are remains and which are imprints. Ask: **Which are the remains of a large animal?** (The photo of large, scattered bones) Ask them what kind of animal might have bones as large as those in the picture. (Children might mention dinosaurs.) Explain that the bones in the picture are mammoth fossils; mammoths are animals that died out about 10,000 years ago. They were early relatives of elephants. Then have children examine the other fossils. Ask them to describe each fossil and to use erasable markers to circle imprints in one color and remains in another color. (One shows the imprint and remains of shells, one is the imprint of a fern leaf, and one is an imprint of a fish.)

• Lead children in a discussion about scientists who study fossils. Ask: **Why are fossils important to scientists?** (Fossils give clues about life on the earth a long time ago, including the sizes, shapes, and appearances of plants and animals from the past.) Encourage children to think about why scientists and they might want to know these things.

Responding To Individual Needs

Children Acquiring English Proficiency   Have children name in their native language and in English the plants or animals in their countries that look like the fossils.

Close

- Discuss why it is easier to tell what an animal looked like from a fossil imprint than from fossil remains. Lead children to conclude that scientists piece together fossil remains without knowing how the whole animal looked or whether all of the remains are there. Ask: **Why are fossils important?** (They provide clues about animals and plants that lived on the earth long ago.)

- **Extend the Activity** Speculate with children how the fossils on the Poster Book page might have been formed, including what might have caused the mammoth to die and how its bones became trapped. In the **multi-age classroom,** you may wish to have some children write reports about finding mammoth bones or dinosaur bones and then share their reports with the class.

Assess

CONCEPT DEVELOPMENT

 Concept Checklist, Assessment Guide p. C73

Use the Concept Checklist to record children's understanding.

- Do children recognize that some fossils are remains of once-living things and some are imprints of once-living things?
- Do children understand that fossils help us learn about life long ago?

 Lesson Assessment, Assessment Guide p. C50

Use the Lesson 3 Assessment to evaluate children's understanding of the lesson concept.

 Group Discussion

Discuss with children whether the plants and animals that lived millions of years ago looked like those that are alive today. Have children tell what scientists of the future might learn from fossils of plants and animals alive today.

 Drawing

Invite each child to draw an imaginary fossil imprint or remains. Then ask each one to explain what the fossil plant or animal looked like when it was alive, where it lived, and when it lived.

Science & Art

SCULPTING WITH CLAY Have children sculpt dinosaur leg bone remains out of clay. Provide them with a skeleton model or picture to refer to for the bone shapes. Small groups could work on different bones in the leg. When children are finished with their "fossils," they can assemble the bones on a table to show a full leg.

 ## Cultural Connection

SHARING DATA Explain that remains of different groups of dinosaurs have been found in many different places. For example, some dinosaur fossils have been found only in North America, while others only in Africa. Ask children who have moved from other parts of the country or other countries to describe what fossil plants and animals a future scientist might find in their native states or countries.

INVESTIGATE FURTHER

In the Science Center

Identifying Types of Fossils

Objective
- **Compare** fossil imprints with fossil remains.

Process Skills
- **Classify** fossils as imprints or remains.
- **Infer** the appearance of a plant or animal from its fossil imprint or remains.

Pacing: 10 minutes

Grouping: Individual

Materials
- Tracing paper
- Activity Card C3
- Fossils used with Activity Card C3
- Various other fossils
- Poster Book p. C3

Procedure
- Ask each child to draw or trace the fossils. When the artwork is completed, have the child label each fossil as remains or imprint. *(classify)*
- Allow children to add outlines in another color to show what they think the whole plant or animal looked like. *(infer)*

Home-School Connection

The Explore at Home activity "Remains to Be Seen" (Teacher Resource Book page C6) invites children to look for pictures of fossils and to categorize them. After children have done the activity with their families and have brought in their sentences or drawings, invite children to share their discoveries with the class.

Make a FINAL ASSESSMENT

Review the *Science Notebook*

Ask questions to determine whether children remember and understand the difference between fossil remains and fossil imprints and why we study fossils.

Return to Baseline Assessment

Display children's responses to the questions asked in Assess Prior Knowledge. Read the responses aloud. Ask children if they would change any of their responses and, if so, how.

Group Discussion

Questions like these can be used to stimulate class discussion.

- **Why is it important to record where fossil imprints and remains were found?** (To know where plants and animals once lived)
- **Why is it important to find plant fossils as well as animal fossils?** (To know what plant-eating animals from long ago ate, what the climate was like then, and how plants may have changed.)

Have children save their work for the portfolio selection process at the end of the unit.

Science & Language Arts

TELLING A STORY Reread the part of *Fossils Tell of Long Ago* that tells about the fish becoming a fossil. Ask children to tell a story in which they take the role of a plant or an animal and explain how they became fossil imprints or remains. Have them begin with the sentences: I was a ___. I lived in ___ about ___ years ago. Children should describe who found them after they became a fossil and how that person found out what they looked like when they were alive.

Looking Ahead

Now that children have learned that fossils show how earlier plants and animals looked, they will learn more about how fossil imprints are made.

LESSON 4

Investigating IMPRINTS

In the **LAST LESSON** children learned that fossils show how earlier plants and animals looked.

In this **LESSON** children learn how fossil imprints are made.

In the **NEXT LESSON** children will learn how handprints and footprints give clues about the size of the person or animal that made them.

Resources

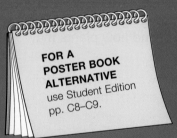

FOR A **POSTER BOOK ALTERNATIVE** use Student Edition pp. C8–C9.

POSTER BOOK p. C4

ACTIVITY CARD C4

TRADE BOOK *Fossils Tell of Long Ago*

Pacing Guide	
Trade Book	15 minutes
Activity Card	20 minutes
Poster Book	20 minutes

Teacher Resource Book
• *Home-School Connection*
• *Science Notebook*
• *Activity Support*
• *Assessment Guide*
• *Unit Project Pages*

Equipment Kit

Lesson Overview

Science Theme: Models
Children simulate making fossil imprints. In these activities, they observe that an imprint is a **model** for a cast of a plant or animal and that there are differences between simulated imprints and fossil imprints.

Project 2061 Benchmarks
• Some kinds of organisms that once lived on earth have completely disappeared, although they were something like others that are alive today.
• A model of something is different from the real thing but can be used to learn something about the real thing.

Concept
• A fossil imprint is formed when a plant or animal leaves a trace, or print, of itself in soil, which gradually turns to rock.

Objectives
• **Compare** imprints of common objects with a fossil imprint.
• **Conclude** that fossil imprints are traces of plants or animals.

Science Words
fossils
fossil imprints
imprints

Activity — Previewing Activity Card C4

Children make imprints of objects and compare them with a fossil imprint. They generalize that although all are imprints, there is a difference between the imprints they made and a fossil imprint.

Grouping
Small groups of 3–4

Materials
• Activity Card C4
• Goggles*
• Hand lens*
• Once-living objects (leaf, twig, shell*)
• Fossil leaf imprint*
• *Science Notebook* p. C20
• Dough*
• Large paper plates*

Advance Preparation
Leaves, twigs, and other once-living objects should be collected ahead of time. Shells are provided in the Equipment Kit.

*In Equipment Kit

Science Background

Fossils are often found in coal. Coal forms when partly rotted plants in shallow swamps harden into peat, which eventually gets covered by sediments. Under pressure, the sediments turn into limestone, sandstone, or shale. The pressure of the rocks turns the peat below into coal, which may contain imprints of plants and animals.

Fossils also form when plants or animals are directly buried in mud. Fossils may be found in concretions, which are masses of rock included in, and different from, surrounding rock.

Older fossils are found in lower layers of rock. Scientists use special tests on bones, rock layers, fossils, and other materials to estimate the true ages of fossils.

Real World Connection Imprints can be made by writing or drawing on hardening concrete or plaster. A Hollywood restaurant preserves hand imprints of famous people. Children may have made imprints of their hands in earlier school years. These are not fossil imprints.

Addressing Misconceptions

Children may believe they are making fossil imprints when they press objects into clay. Explain that fossils are formed from living things that lived long, long ago.

Books for Children

***Dinosaur Bones* by Aliki (Crowell, 1988).** Discusses how scientists, studying fossil remains, provide information on how dinosaurs lived millions of years ago. (PreK–Grade 3)

***Dinosaurs Walked Here, and Other Stories Fossils Tell* by Patricia Lauber (Bradbury Press, 1987).** Discusses how fossilized remains of plants and animals reveal characteristics of the prehistoric world. Good information on imprints may be found on pages 10 and 11 in chapter one. (Grades 2–5)

Setting the Stage

Using the Trade Book

Read aloud *Fossils Tell of Long Ago*. Have children compare the imprints of the fish and the flying animal. Ask: **How are these imprints different?** (The whole image of the flying animal is preserved but only the imprint of the fish bones remains.)

Point out the two halves of the rock on page 15. Ask: **What happened to the animal?** Reread aloud what the children in the story are saying. Help children compare the rock halves to cookie-mold imprints and recall how the baker makes cookies with different shapes and details. Discuss the analogy between the molded cookies and using imprint molds to reproduce the shape.

Display page 28 and ask children to explain how to make an imprint. Ask: **Are these children making fossil imprints? Why not?** (Only imprints of long-ago plants and animals are real fossil imprints.)

 **Activity** **Assess Prior Knowledge**

Making a Baseline Assessment
Ask: **What is a fossil imprint? How is one made? Can we make fossil imprints? Do imprints look exactly like what made them? What can you tell about a plant or animal from its imprint?** Record responses on chart paper and save them for comparison in Make a Final Assessment at the end of the lesson.

Using the ACTIVITY CARD

Comparing Imprints

Activity C4

1. Flatten a piece of dough on a paper plate.

2. Press each object into the dough and carefully remove it.

3. Look closely at each imprint. Record what you see.

4. Compare your imprints with a fossil imprint.

Think! How are your imprints different from the fossil imprint?

Organize

Objective

- **Compare** imprints of common objects with a fossil imprint.

Process Skills

- **Make a model** of a fossil imprint to understand how fossil imprints are made.
- **Observe** how an object is different from its imprint.

Pacing: 20 minutes

Grouping: Small groups of 3–4

Materials
- Activity Card C4
- Goggles
- Dough
- Large paper plates
- Hand lens
- Once-living objects (leaf, twig, shell)
- Fossil imprint
- *Science Notebook* p. C20

Safety: Have children wear goggles. Caution them to keep objects and hands away from their faces.

Guide

- **Warm-Up** At this time, make sure children understand the words **fossils** (preserved evidence of former life), **fossil imprints** (fossilized impressions) and **imprints** (impressions). Have them recall the fossil imprints they had observed earlier.
- In step 1, have children shape the dough on a paper plate so it is deeper than any of the objects and wide enough to take three impressions.
- In step 2, caution children as they make the imprint not to press so hard that they break the object or get their fingerprints in the clay. *(make a model)*
- In step 3, have children look through the hand lens and draw what they see in their *Science Notebook* page C20. Ask: **How are the imprints and the objects alike and different?** (The imprints are like the objects in details and just the opposite in their shapes. The imprints go deepest into the clay where the objects stick out farthest.) *(observe)*
- In step 4, have them compare each imprint they made with the fossil imprint and write words describing the differences. Point out to children that they did not make a fossil imprint; rather they *made a model* of a fossil imprint. Fossil imprints were formed a long time ago from things that lived long ago.

Responding To Individual Needs

Gifted and Talented Children   Before children make the imprints in the dough, ask them to imagine what the imprints will look like. Have them draw what they imagine. After they make their imprints, have children draw how the imprints look and compare them with what they imagined. You may wish to have children make their drawings on copies of the Activity Support blackline master titled "Prediction/Result" (Teacher Resource Book page C33).

 Expected Results

- Did children handle the objects carefully as they made the imprints?
- Did they use the hand lens properly to look for differences between the imprints they made and the fossil imprints?

 Process Skills Checklist, Assessment Guide p. C68

Use the Process Skills Checklist to record children's performance.

- Did children *make a model* imprint to understand how fossil imprints are made?
- Did children *observe* how an object is different from its imprint and how different objects made different imprints?

 Group Skills Checklist, Assessment Guide p. C69

Use the Group Skills Checklist to record children's performance.

- Did children *take initiative* to begin the activity?
- Did they *communicate clearly* the differences among the imprints they made?
- Did they *discuss* how their imprints were different from the fossil imprint?

Close

⬛ Have children compare their imprints to see if they look alike. As an alternative, have children guess which object made each imprint. Ask: **How is making an imprint in dough different from the way the fossil imprint was made?** (The modern objects are still here, but the ancient objects are gone; the imprints were made purposely, but the fossils were made accidentally.)

- **Think!** Answer: Children's imprints are different from fossil imprints in appearance, size, depth, and age.

⬛ **Extend the Activity** Ask: **How could you use the imprint to make a model of the object?** (Fill the imprint with water and freeze it.) Have children fill the imprints with colored water and then freeze them to make models of the objects used.

 **USES DIFFERENT GROUPING**

Pacing: 20 minutes
Grouping: Whole class
Materials

- Goggles
- Dough
- Large paper plates
- Once-living objects (leaf, twig, shell)
- Fossil imprint

Procedure

- Have all children observe, and if possible touch, the three objects and the fossil imprint.
- Select a different child to make an imprint of each object.
- Have children decide which is the real fossil imprint and then match each object with its imprint.
- Help children compare the "made" imprints with the fossil imprint and reach a consensus on the differences.

LESSON 4

Using the POSTER BOOK

Look at the fossil footprints.
What do the footprints tell us about the animals that made them?

Use with Lesson 4.
Teaching Guide page C44.

Earth Through Time C4

POSTER BOOK PAGE

Organize

Objective

• **Conclude** that fossil imprints are traces of plants or animals.

Process Skills

• **Infer** information about the animal that made a fossil footprint.

• **Measure** a child's hand and a dinosaur's footprint.

Pacing: 20 minutes

Grouping: Whole class

Materials
• Poster Book p. C4
• String

Using the Student Edition: You may wish to use Student Edition pages C8–C9 to extend or replace the Poster Book lesson.

Guide

• **Warm Up** Discuss whether children have ever noticed their footprints in sand or mud. Ask them to describe their footprints. Display Poster Book page C4 and explain that these footprints are in stone and are called fossil footprints. Dinosaur footprints are sometimes called dinosaur tracks.

⬛ **Poster Book** Help children compare the sizes of the pictured child's hand and the large dinosaur footprint. They can use string to *measure* how many times the child's hand fits into the fossil footprint. Ask: **How much bigger than the child do you think the animal was that made the footprint?** (Help children see the relationship between the size of their own feet and their own height and *infer* that foot size can provide clues to body size.)

⬛ Ask: **What do the footprints tell us about the animals that made them?** (Size and shape of the animals' feet) **Would all dinosaurs make the same kind of footprints? Why not?** (No; dinosaurs were different sizes and had different shapes, some had claws; some walked on two feet.) **How could you tell what kind of animal made footprints found in the snow or mud?** (By examining the size and shape of the footprints)

👤 Responding To Individual Needs

Visual Activity Display the dinosaur pictures at the end of *How Big Were the Dinosaurs?* Ask children to describe how the size and shape of the dinosaurs' feet and their number of toes would make the footprints different. In the **multi-age classroom**, you may wish to have some children draw pictures of how they think the tracks of some of the dinosaurs might look.

**Concept Checklist,
Assessment Guide p. C74**

Use the Concept Checklist to record children's understanding.

- Do children recognize that a fossil imprint forms when a plant or animal leaves a trace, or imprint, of itself in sediment, which gradually turns to rock?
- Do children understand that a fossil footprint gives information about the animal that made it?

 **Lesson Assessment,
Assessment Guide p. C51**

Use the Lesson 4 Assessment to evaluate children's understanding of the lesson concept.

Close

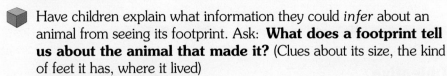

Have children explain what information they could *infer* about an animal from seeing its footprint. Ask: **What does a footprint tell us about the animal that made it?** (Clues about its size, the kind of feet it has, where it lived)

- **Extend the Activity** Have children find pictures of animals in books. Ask volunteers to describe what each animal's footprint would look like and what it would tell about the size of the animal and how it walks.

 Discussion Starters

Ask: **How do you make an imprint?** Have children describe the procedure. **Can you make a fossil imprint? Why not?** Lead children to conclude that they can't; fossil imprints are traces of life from long ago. Even imprints in cement are not fossils.

Debate

Debate the topic: **Would imprints of houses or cars be fossils in the future?** Houses and cars are not alive, so do not fit the definition of *fossil*. Children may point out that houses and cars could be future evidence of "former" life.

STS **Science, Technology & Society**

INTERPRETING DATA

Explain that museums often hire scientists to find and study fossils. They record where fossils were found and figure out how old the fossils are and what the plant or animal looked like. Ask: **Why is this work important?** Help children conclude that we can learn what animals and plants lived at the same times and what the earth was like at different times in the past.

 Integrating the Sciences

EXPLORING ROCKS

Tell children that scientists use some kinds of fossils (called index fossils) to learn about how old certain rocks are. If scientists know how long ago a fossil plant or animal lived, they know that the rock in which the fossil was found formed at about the same time. Ask: **If you found a dinosaur fossil in a rock, what would you know about the rock?** (The rock was formed when dinosaurs were alive.)

INVESTIGATE FURTHER

In the Science Center

Identifying Different Footprints

Objective

- **Conclude** that fossil imprints are traces of plants or animals.

Process Skill

- **Observe** that dinosaur footprints give clues to which dinosaurs made the footprints.

Pacing: 20 minutes

Grouping: Pairs

Materials

- Drawing paper
- Crayons
- Models used with Activity Card C1

Procedure

- Direct each child to select a dinosaur secretly and draw the imprints (same size and shape) that the dinosaur's feet would make.
- Have children exchange papers and *observe* the footprints to identify which dinosaur their partner chose.
- If either child chooses incorrectly, children should describe how the drawing made by the child differs from the imprints the dinosaur would actually make.
- When all children are finished, help them conclude that dinosaur footprints are imprints of the feet of particular dinosaurs.

Home-School Connection

The Explore at Home activity "Footprints" (Teacher Resource Book page C7) invites children to trace outlines of various feet. After children have done the activity with their families and have brought in the foot outlines they made, invite children to share them with the class.

Cultural Connection

SHARING FOSSILS   In 1993, the government of Niger, Africa, let scientists from the United States and Canada look for dinosaur bones. Scientists share the fossils they find. They make molds and give copies of bones to others. Ask: **Why should scientists share what they find?** (Lead children to conclude that when scientists share discoveries and build on each other's work we learn more about what life was like long ago.)

Make a
FINAL ASSESSMENT

 Review the *Science Notebook*

Ask questions to see whether children understand what a fossil imprint is and how one is formed.

Return to Baseline Assessment

Display children's responses to the Assess Prior Knowledge questions and read them aloud. Allow children to make changes and add information learned in the lesson. Make sure they understand that modern imprints are not fossils and that imprints contain information about the original life-form.

Discussion Starters

Ask questions like the following to stimulate class discussion:

- **What would scientists know if they found many footprints of the same kind of dinosaur together?** (The dinosaurs lived or traveled together.)
- **What might scientists think if they found footprints of different dinosaurs together?** (That they may have lived at the same time near each other)

Have children save their work for the portfolio selection process at the end of the unit.

Looking Ahead

Now that children have learned how fossil imprints and footprints are made, they will learn more about how handprints and footprints give clues about the sizes of the animals that made them.

LESSON 5

Investigating

HANDPRINTS AND FOOTPRINTS

In the **LAST LESSON** children learned how fossil imprints are made.

In this **LESSON** children learn how handprints and footprints give clues about the size of the person or animal that made them.

In the **NEXT LESSON** children will learn that fossil bones give clues about the size and shape of animals that lived long ago.

Resources

FOR A POSTER BOOK ALTERNATIVE use Student Edition pp. C10–C11.

POSTER BOOK p. C5 AND PICTURE CARDS C5, C6, C7, C8, C9

ACTIVITY CARD C5

TRADE BOOK *Fossils Tell of Long Ago*

Pacing Guide	
Trade Book	15 minutes
Activity Card	20 minutes
Poster Book & Picture Cards	20 minutes

Teacher Resource Book
• *Home-School Connection*
• *Science Notebook*
• *Activity Support*
• *Assessment Guide*
• *Unit Project Pages*

Equipment Kit

Lesson Overview

Science Theme: Models
Children make handprints to simulate how fossil footprints are made. They observe that an imprint is a **model** of a handprint or a footprint.

Project 2061 Benchmark
• A model of something is different from the real thing but can be used to learn something about the real thing.

Concept
• Dinosaur fossil footprints are clues to the size of a dinosaur and the size and shape of its feet.

Objectives
• **Infer** the sizes of people from imprints of their hands.
• **Conclude** that dinosaur fossil footprints give clues about the sizes of dinosaurs.

Science Words
footprint   handprint

 **Activity** *Previewing* **Activity Card C5**

Children measure their own handprints and a mystery handprint and generalize that handprints provide clues about a person's size.

Grouping
Small groups of 3–4

Materials
• Activity Card C5
• Goggles*
• Flour, salt, water
• Large mixing bowl
• Mixing spoon
• Measuring cup
• *Science Notebook*   p. C21
• Plastic wrap
• Airtight container
• 12" ruler
• Large paper plates*
• Petroleum jelly (optional)

Advance Preparation
To make dough, combine 10 c flour, 2½ c salt, and 4½ c water. Mix thoroughly and knead to remove any lumps. Divide dough into six, form each part into a ball, wrap balls in plastic and store them in an airtight container. Use one of the balls to make a "mystery" handprint of a staff member known to children and mark it for later identification. Use the other 5 balls for the children's handprints and, if possible, for another mystery handprint of a baby or a toddler.

* *In Equipment Kit*

 Pressed for Time?
This lesson targets a key concept in this unit. Use this lesson and Lessons 1, 2, 3, 6, and 9 if your teaching time is limited.

Science Background

Fossil footprints give clues about which dinosaurs lived in the same place at the same time. When scientists found groups of the same kinds of dinosaur footprints, they realized that dinosaurs were not solitary but traveled in packs or herds. Footprints of baby and adult dinosaurs together show that dinosaurs cared for their young.

Footprints also show that dinosaurs' feet lay flat on the ground to support the body weight and allow them to move. By knowing the length of dinosaurs' legs and measuring the distance between footprints, scientists have concluded that some dinosaurs could move as fast as 30 miles per hour or even more.

Real World Connection Fingerprints and footprints are often used in investigations for identification.

Books for Children

Discover Dinosaurs: Become a Dinosaur Detective by Chris McGowan (Addison-Wesley, 1992). Hands-on activities present information about dinosaurs and show how paleontologists have learned about prehistoric creatures. Modify activities for the Science Center and read aloud from the text for additional information. (Grades 3–5)

Hunting the Dinosaur and Other Prehistoric Animals by Dougal Dixon (Gareth Stevens, 1987). This book examines how paleontologists discover, study, classify, reconstruct, and restore the fossil remains of many kinds of dinosaurs and other prehistoric animals. Use with advanced or motivated students or read aloud information on fossils to all students. (Grades 3–5)

Let's Go Dinosaur Tracking by M. Schlein (HarperCollins, 1991). Explores the many different kinds of tracks dinosaurs left behind and what they reveal about the dinosaurs themselves. (Grades 2–5)

Setting the
Stage

Using the Trade Book

Read aloud pages 28–30 of *Fossils Tell of Long Ago.* 🔳 Ask: **If you made an imprint of your foot, why wouldn't it be a fossil?** (A fossil footprint is very old.) Invite children who made handprints in past years to bring them in and compare hand sizes now and then. 🔳 Ask: **What would someone in the future know about you from the imprints of your hands and feet?** (Size; number of fingers, thumbs, and toes; number of hands and feet.) Read page 31 aloud. Discuss what the boy and girl are saying and what it's possible to know. Be sure children understand you could not know the things the girl is describing.

Display the footprints shown in *How Big Were the Dinosaurs?* Ask: **How big are these footprints?** (Help children conclude that they need something to compare them with, as on the next page of the book.)

Activity Assess Prior Knowledge

Making a Baseline Assessment
Ask: **What happens to our footprints in sand or mud? How do you know the size of a handprint or footprint? What does the size of a handprint or footprint tell you?** Record responses on chart paper and save them for comparison in Make a Final Assessment at the end of the lesson.

LESSON 5

Using the
ACTIVITY CARD

Comparing Handprints

Activity C5

1. Flatten dough on a paper plate.

2. Spread your fingers apart. Carefully make a handprint in the dough.

3. Measure your handprint. Record the measurements.

4. Measure the mystery handprint. Record the measurements.

5. Compare your handprint to the mystery handprint.

Think! What clues does each handprint give you?

Earth Through Time

Organize

Objective

- **Infer** the sizes of people from imprints of their hands.

Process Skills

- **Make** and **use models** of hands by making handprints.
- **Measure** the handprints.

Pacing: 20 minutes

Grouping: Small groups of 3–4

Materials

- Activity Card C5
- Goggles
- Dough
- Paper plate
- Ruler
- Mystery handprint
- *Science Notebook* p. C21

For Best Results: Have children moisten their hands with petroleum jelly before laying them on the dough so the dough won't stick to their hands.

Safety: Have children wear goggles. Caution them to keep objects and hands away from their faces and not to eat the dough.

Guide

🔲 **Warm-Up** Before children start the activity, have those in each group put their hands together palm-to-palm to see that their hands are nearly but not exactly the same size. Ask: **Will your hands get bigger as you get older? How do you know?** (Adults' hands are bigger than children's hands, but adults' hands are not all the same size, either.)

- In step 1, have children flatten the dough so they can make a **handprint** on it by pressing a hand on the dough.

- In step 2, have children spread the fingers of one hand in the air before they place their hands on the dough. *(make a model)* Have children put their names and the date on their handprints. They may wish to take them home, and their families may want to keep them.

- In step 3, have children *use the model* they have just made. They should use a ruler to *measure* the length of their handprint from the wrist to the end of the middle finger and the width from one side of the handprint to the other side. Direct them to record the measurements on *Science Notebook* page C21.

- In step 4, have children measure the same distances on the mystery handprints as they did on their own handprint and record the measurements.

- In step 5, have children compare the measurements of the two handprints.

👤 Responding To Individual Needs

Visual Activity   Have children identify other details of a hand, such as fingerprints, lines on the palm, and the number of segments of each finger.

 Expected Results

- Did children make handprints by pressing their hands firmly on the dough?
- Did children use the ruler correctly to measure the length and width of the handprints?
- Did they compare the measurements of their handprints and the mystery handprints accurately?

 Process Skills Checklist, Assessment Guide p. C68

Use the Process Skills Checklist to record children's performance.

- Did children *make* and *use models* of hands by making handprints?
- Did children *measure* the length and width of the handprints?

Group Skills Checklist, Assessment Guide p. C69

Use the Group Skills Checklist to record children's performance.

- Did children *take initiative* to begin the activity?
- Did they *communicate clearly* their ideas about the mystery handprint?

Close

- Have children use the sizes of the handprints to guess whether the mystery handprint belongs to a baby, a small child, or an adult, and to explain their answers.
- **Think!** Answer: Help children list clues such as size of person, shape of hand, and number of fingers.
- **Extend the Activity** Have children measure their height and then compare the measurements of their handprints with the measurements of their heights. Have children put this data in chart form.

 Alternate **Activity** **Uses less time**

Pacing: 10 minutes
Grouping: Pairs
Materials

- Mystery handprints
- Paper and pencils

Procedure

- Have the partners trace one of each other's hands. After the traced picture has been labeled with the date and child's name, have children measure their partner's hand outline with a ruler. Have them measure the length from the wrist to the end of the middle finger and the width from side to side.

- Hand out one of the mystery handprints prepared in advance for Activity Card C5.
- Discuss with children how the mystery handprint was made. Point out that it is an imprint.
- Ask: **Does this handprint belong to a baby, toddler, child, or adult? How can you tell?** (Children's answers should recognize that as a person gets older, his or her hand increases in size until adulthood is reached.)

Using the POSTER BOOK & PICTURE CARDS

Look at the dinosaurs and the footprints.
Match each footprint with a dinosaur.
What can you learn about each dinosaur from its footprint?

Use with Lesson 5, Teaching Guide page C52.

Earth Through Time C5

POSTER BOOK PAGE

---

❶ Saltasaurus (sôl tə sôr′əs)　❷ Tyrannosaurus (tə ran′ə sôr əs)　❸ Parksosaurus (pärks′ō sôr əs)　❹ Hypacrosaurus (hī päk′rō sôr əs)

❺ Panoplosaurus (pə näp′lō sôr əs)　❻ Panoplosaurus footprint　❼ Hypacrosaurus footprint　❽ Parksosaurus footprint

❾ Saltasaurus footprint　❿ Tyrannosaurus footprint

Organize

Objective

- **Conclude** that dinosaur fossil footprints give clues about the sizes of dinosaurs.

Process Skill

- **Infer** which footprint belongs to each dinosaur.

Pacing: 20 minutes

Grouping: Whole class

Materials

- Poster Book p. C5
- Picture Cards C5, C6, C7, C8, C9
  (See backs of Picture Cards for questions, facts, and related activities.)
- Erasable marker

For Best Results: If you use an erasable marker on the Poster Book page, wipe it off immediately after the lesson.

Using the Student Edition: You may wish to use Student Edition pages C10–C11 to extend or replace the Poster Book lesson.

Guide

- **Warm-Up** Describe a mystery scenario to children in which a burglar has left **footprints** in a muddy area in the backyard. Have children speculate what detectives might learn about the burglar by studying the footprints. (Size of the burglar's feet and shape of the burglar's shoes.)
- **Poster Book** Display Poster Book page C5. Tell children that the artist drew all these different dinosaurs together on an imaginary walk in order to show the differences in their legs and feet. Have children compare the dinosaurs, paying close attention to their feet.
- Ask: **How are the dinosaurs' feet different?** (The feet differ in size, shape, and number of toes. On some dinosaurs, the front feet are different from the hind feet.)
- Have volunteers use an erasable marker to match each dinosaur with its appropriate footprint. *(infer)* Ask children to explain their matches.
- **Picture Cards** Display the five picture cards and have children examine them and discuss the different characteristics of each dinosaur, paying particular attention to the dinosaurs' feet. Ask: **How are the feet of each dinosaur different?** (Shape, number of toes.) Explain that the dinosaurs on the Picture Cards have not been drawn proportionally to each other and there is no nearby common object on each card to help determine their relative sizes. Help children to match the dinosaurs on the Picture Cards to the dinosaurs on the Poster Book Page.

👤 Responding To Individual Needs

<u>Gifted and Talented Children</u>　Provide children with pictures of animal tracks from books or magazines. After they have examined the pictures of several animals' tracks, ask them to draw footprints that other animals might make. Ask them to exchange papers and try to identify each footprint.

C5: Tyrannosaurus
C6: Parksosaurus
C7: Hypacrosaurus
C8: Panoplosaurus
C9: Saltasaurus

Close

 Ask children to imagine they have found three sets of dinosaur footprints. Have them explain what they would look for, count, and measure before they decide which footprint belongs to which dinosaur. Ask: **How can you tell which footprint goes with each dinosaur?** (Size of footprint, number of toes, shape of toes)

 Extend the Activity Have children speculate how scientists might be able to identify a dinosaur if they found footprints and no dinosaur bones. In the **multi-age classroom**, you may wish to have some children make their own posters showing other dinosaurs and their footprints. Then have them ask their classmates to identify which footprint belongs to which dinosaur.

Assess
CONCEPT DEVELOPMENT

 Concept Checklist, Assessment Guide p. C75

Use the Concept Checklist to record children's understanding.

- Do children understand that handprints can tell something about the person who made them?
- Do children recognize that scientists study fossil footprints to identify dinosaurs and learn about them?

Lesson Assessment, Assessment Guide p. C52

Use the Lesson 5 Assessment to evaluate children's understanding of the lesson concept.

Discussion Starters

- **Why might future scientists be confused if they found footprints from a basketball game?** (Many different footprints in random order)
- **What could they tell about the players? Tell how they could do that?** (They could tell the sizes of the players' feet by measuring the footprints and then they could infer how tall the players were.)

 Science & Music

IMAGINING SOUNDS

Have children pretend to be different dinosaurs in a marching band. Children should determine what kind of sounds they think the dinosaurs might make and how light or heavy their footsteps might be as they march in a dinosaur parade.

 **Science & Social Studies**

DRAWING A MAP

Ask children to imagine they are scientists in the future. They have just discovered some fossil footprints. Have children draw maps to show where they found the footprints. Maps should include the footprints and one or two features in the imagined scene (a building, for example). Remind children to include an object to use for comparing size.

INVESTIGATE FURTHER

UNIT PROJECT LINK

Dinosaur Place: Making Tracks

Have each child select a dinosaur listed on the Dinosaur Chart and draw on the Unit Project page an outline of its footprint.

Then invite children to make dinosaur footprint stamps. Using their sketches as guidelines, have children use a metal spoon to carve the shape of the footprint on half of a raw potato.

Then have children use the footprint stamp and tempera paint spread on a sponge to make a series of tracks across a piece of bulletin-board paper. Have children label each set of tracks and mount them around the room.

Use Unit Project page C99 in the Teacher Resource Book with this activity.

In the Science Center

Making Dinosaur Model Footprints

Objective
- **Conclude** that dinosaur fossil footprints give clues about the sizes of dinosaurs.

Process Skills
- **Use models** of dinosaurs to make dinosaur footprints.
- **Infer** which model was used to make each footprint.

Pacing: 20 minutes

Grouping: Pairs

Materials
- Models from Activity Card C1
- Dough

Procedure
- Invite each child to secretly select a dinosaur model and press one of its feet onto a flattened piece of dough.
- Children should exchange footprints with their partners and try to identify the dinosaur model that was used to make each. *(use a model, infer)*
- Ask children to explain how they made their identifications.

Home-School Connection

The Explore at Home activity "Handprint Cookies" (Teacher Resource Book page C8) invites children to make handprint cookies. After children have done the activity with their families and have brought in their handprint cookies, invite children to share with the class how they made the cookies.

Make a FINAL ASSESSMENT

 Review the *Science Notebook*

Ask questions to see whether children understand that fossil footprints can give clues to the sizes and shapes of dinosaurs.

 Return to Baseline Assessment

Display children's responses to the Assess Prior Knowledge questions. Read them aloud and let children make changes or add information they learned in the lesson.

 Group Discussion

Ask children what scientists could learn from adult and baby dinosaur footprints going in the same direction. Explain that scientists once thought dinosaurs lived alone. From fossil footprints, they learned that some dinosaurs traveled together and cared for their young.

 In My Opinion

Have children imagine that scientists found some 5-inch dinosaur fossil footprints about 3 feet apart. Have children explain what size they think the dinosaur would be and why they think so. Help them explain that the distance between the prints means that the dinosaur either had long legs or was running.

Have children save their work for the portfolio selection process at the end of the unit.

 ## Science & Math

GRAPHING DATA

Have children collect the handprint measurements they made earlier in the lesson and put them in size order according to the length from wrist to end of middle finger. Help children create a bar graph showing the number of children with each size hand, using copies of Activity Support blackline master titled "2-cm Grid" (Teacher Resource Book page C31). Create a second graph of children's heights. Have the class compare the two graphs.

Looking Ahead

Now that children have learned that handprints and footprints give clues about the sizes of the animals that made them, they will learn that fossil bones give other clues about dinosaurs' sizes and shapes.

LESSON 6

Investigating FOSSIL REMAINS

| In the **LAST LESSON** children learned how handprints and footprints give clues about the size of the person or animal that made them. | In this **LESSON** children learn that fossil bones give clues about the size and shape of animals that lived long ago. | In the **NEXT LESSON** children will learn what teeth reveal about a dinosaur. |

Resources

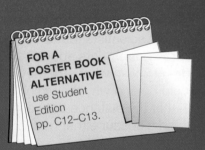

FOR A POSTER BOOK ALTERNATIVE use Student Edition pp. C12–C13.

POSTER BOOK p. C6 AND PICTURE CARDS C10, C11, C12, C13

ACTIVITY CARD C6

TRADE BOOK *How Big Were the Dinosaurs?*

Pacing Guide

Pacing Guide	
Trade Book	15 minutes
Activity Card	20 minutes
Poster Book & Picture Cards	20 minutes

Teacher Resource Book
- *Home-School Connection*
- *Science Notebook*
- *Activity Support*
- *Assessment Guide*
- *Unit Project Pages*

Videotape   **Equipment Kit**

Lesson Overview

Science Theme: Models
Children simulate searching for fossil remains. In these activities, they observe that remains are full-size clues to the size and shape of an animal. Children **model** digging up fossil remains.

Project 2061 Benchmark
- A model of something is different from the real thing but can be used to learn something about the real thing.

Concept
- Fossil bones give clues to sizes and shapes of dinosaurs.

Objectives
- **Infer** the size of an animal from its remains.
- **Model** scientific behavior by digging up buried remains.

Science Words
fossil remains   remains

Activity Previewing **Activity Card C6**

Children search for chicken bones and rat bones in sand and generalize that scientists must be very careful when retrieving fossil remains and that remains of bones can give clues about the size of animals.

Grouping
Small groups of 3–4

Materials
- Activity Card C6
- Goggles*
- Newspapers
- Tray*
- Sand*
- *Science Notebook* p. C22
- Plastic spoons*
- 2 chicken bones*
- 2 rat bones*
- Large paper plates*

Advance Preparation
Prepare a tray of sand for each group. Carefully hide the two chicken bones together and the two rat bones together in the sand. Try to place the bones in the correct leg position for each animal. Do not tell children what they will uncover in the sand.

* In Equipment Kit

Pressed for Time?
This lesson targets a key concept in this unit. Use this lesson and Lessons 1, 2, 3, 5, and 9 if your teaching time is limited.

Science Background

Fossil dinosaur bones often become visible when the ground where they are buried is eroded by water and wind. Sometimes only small fragments are visible and scientists must visualize what may lie below ground.

Scientists use shovels, pick axes, drills, and air hoses to clear away rock and soil. Near the bones, they use brushes, hammers and chisels, and small picks. Sometimes they carefully spray liquid to wash soil away. Because bones can break or turn to powder when they are moved, they are covered with paper or aluminum foil and wrapped in burlap covered with plaster.

Addressing Misconceptions

Children may believe that fossil bones are connected as a skeleton would be. Explain that it's rare to find many bones connected to each other. Fossil bones are usually scattered.

Books for Children

***Dinosaur Babies* by Lucille Recht Penner (Random House, 1991).** This title describes the characteristics and behavior of baby dinosaurs. (PreK–Grade 1)

***Discovering Dinosaur Babies* by Miriam Schlein (Four Winds Press, 1991).** An explanation of what paleontologists have been able to determine about how the different varieties of dinosaurs cared for their young. (Grades 1–5)

***The News About Dinosaurs* by Patricia Lauber (Bradbury Press, 1990).** This informative introduction to dinosaurs includes information on dinosaur babies. (Grades 1–5)

Setting the Stage

Using the Trade Book

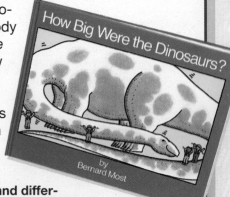

Read aloud pages about dinosaurs' length and sizes of body parts from *How Big Were the Dinosaurs?* Ask children how scientists know a dinosaur's length. Help them conclude that scientists study the sizes of the bones and piece them together to calculate length.

■ Ask: **How are bones in a chicken and a turkey alike and different?** (Help children conclude that both have wings and two legs; chicken bones would be smaller than turkey bones.) Explain to children that chicken bones and turkey bones are remains, but not fossil remains.

■ At some sites, bones of dinosaurs and other animals are found together. Ask: **What might cause scientists to put the wrong head on a dinosaur?** (Lead children to conclude that it may be difficult to tell which bones belong to which animal.)

Activity 👋 Assess Prior Knowledge

Making a Baseline Assessment
Ask: **Why are scientists so careful when they dig up fossil bones? Why do they record where each fossil was buried? How do they know which bones belong to each dinosaur? How do they know the size of each dinosaur?** Record responses on chart paper and save them for comparison in Make a Final Assessment at the end of the lesson.

Using Technology

Videotape: *Digging Up Dinosaurs*
After completing Activity Card C6, review with children the videotape *Digging Up Dinosaurs.* Discuss with them the importance of work done by paleontologists.

Using the ACTIVITY CARD

Finding Remains in Sand

Activity C6

1. Pretend you're a scientist digging for animal remains.
2. Dig carefully in the sand, one spoonful at a time.
3. Place sand on one of the paper plates.
4. Place any remains you find on another paper plate.
5. Record your findings.

Think! What can you learn from the remains you found?

Earth Through Time

Organize

Objectives

- **Infer** the size of an animal from its remains.
- **Model** scientific behavior by digging up buried remains.

Process Skills

- **Collect, record,** and **interpret data** in order to model scientific behavior.
- **Observe** that buried remains may be used to identify animals that left them behind.

Pacing: 20 minutes

Grouping: Small groups of 3–4

Materials

- Activity Card C6
- Goggles
- Newspapers
- Tray of sand
- Plastic spoons
- Large paper plates
- *Science Notebook* p. C22

Safety: Have children wear goggles. Caution them not to get any sand near their faces and not to place any remains they find in their mouths. Also caution them to handle the sand carefully and not to throw it.

Guide

- **Warm-Up** Before children start the activity, discuss what they might find by digging in the sand. Explain that they will model what scientists do when they dig for dinosaur bones. Be sure children understand that fossil dinosaur bones are the **fossil remains** of a dinosaur.

- In steps 1 and 2, help children decide where to start digging. Help them conclude that they should begin in one corner and proceed systematically across the tray.

- In step 3, have children *observe* each spoonful of sand carefully before deciding whether there are any **remains** in it.

- In step 4, have children *collect* the bones on the plate in the position in which they found them in the sand and explain why this might be important.

- In step 5, have children *record* what they found in their *Science Notebooks*. The drawings of the bones should be the same sizes as the actual bones. Ask: **Do you think the bones came from more than one animal? Tell why.** (Two animals; one set of bones is larger than the other) **What part of the animals do you think the bones came from?** (Legs) *(interpret data)* **Were the animals that the bones came from large or small?** (Both were small, but one was smaller than the other.) **What animals do you think the bones came from?** (Small animals—a chicken and a rat)

Responding To Individual Needs

Tactile/Kinesthetic Activity Have two trays with bones hidden in them available for children to experiment with—in one tray have sand, in the other have damp gravel. Also have an assortment of small tools such as small hammers, picks, and brushes. Have children experiment with carefully using the tools the way they think scientists might use them.

 Expected Results

- Did children dig in a systematic pattern, showing that they understood that the position of the bones might be important?
- Did they look carefully at the contents of each spoonful before deciding whether there were any remains?

 Process Skills Checklist, Assessment Guide p. C68

Use the Process Skills Checklist to record children's performance.

- Did children *collect, record,* and *interpret data* while digging for animal remains?
- Did they *observe* that the buried remains were from two different-sized animals?

 Group Skills Checklist, Assessment Guide p. C69

Use the Group Skills Checklist to record children's performance.

- Did children *encourage* each other to participate in the activity?
- Did they *share the tasks* of the activity?
- Did they *discuss* what they learned about the animals from the bones they found?

Close

- Have children speculate why scientists usually do not dig up complete skeletons of dinosaurs. (Children might say that the missing bones might have been separated from the others and weren't buried in the sand in the same place.)
- **Think!** Answer: Children should infer that there were bones from two different animals and something about the sizes of the animals.
- **Extend the Activity** Have children draw pictures of how they think the legs of the animals looked.

 **Alternate Activity** **USES DIFFERENT MATERIALS**

Pacing: 20 minutes
Grouping: Small groups of 3–4
Materials

- Activity Card C6
- Tray of sand
- Dinosaur skeleton model
- Goggles
- Newspapers
- Plastic spoons
- Large paper plates
- *Science Notebook* p. C22

Procedure

- Place the pieces of a dinosaur skeleton model in the tray of sand. Have children complete the steps for Activity Card C6, taking turns doing the digging and inspecting the sand.
- Ask: **What can you tell about the dinosaur from the model remains you dug up?** (Children might mention the shapes of dinosaurs.)
- After they have finished digging, allow the children to try to assemble the dinosaur skeleton.

Using the POSTER BOOK & PICTURE CARDS

A dinosaur's bones give us clues to its shape and size. Which dinosaur did each bone come from? Tell why you think so.

Use with Lesson 6, Teaching Guide page C60.

Earth Through Time C6

POSTER BOOK PAGE

❶ Stenonychosaurus (sten ō nīk'o sôr əs) 6½' ❷ Ankylosaurus (an kī lə sôr'əs) 33' ❸ Ouranosaurus (oo rän ə sôr'əs) 23'
❹ Skull of Ankylosaurus ❺ Skull of Ouranosaurus ❻ Skull of Stenonychosaurus ❼ Foot of Ouranosaurus
❽ Foot of Stenonychosaurus ❾ Foot of Ankylosaurus

Organize

Objective

- Infer the size of an animal from its remains.

Process Skill

- Make hypotheses about which bones belong to which dinosaurs.

Pacing: 20 minutes

Grouping: Whole class

Materials

- Poster Book p. C6
- Picture Cards C10, C11, C12, C13
  (See backs of Picture Cards for questions, facts, and related activities.)
- Erasable marker

For Best Results: If you use an erasable marker on the Poster Book page, wipe it off immediately after the lesson.

Using the Student Edition: You may wish to use Student Edition pages C12–C13 to extend or replace the Poster Book lesson.

Guide

- **Warm-Up** Have children relate their experiences with putting together jigsaw puzzles. Explain that in a similar way, scientists piece together the skeletal remains of dinosaurs to get a "picture" of what they looked like.
- **Poster Book** Display Poster Book page C6. Ask: **How are the three dinosaurs different?** (Have children compare the dinosaurs' shapes, number of legs, and other characteristics.) **How do bones give clues about a dinosaur's size and shape?** (Bones give clues about the length of legs, tails, and necks, shape of the head, and shape of feet. Small dinosaurs had small bones, big dinosaurs had big bones.)
- Have children *make a hypothesis* about which dinosaur each bone on the Poster Book page came from and give their reasons (sizes and shapes). Have them use an erasable marker to draw a line from each bone to the matching dinosaur.
- **Picture Cards** Show the children the Picture Cards, discussing each one as you do. Point out that they can judge the size of each dinosaur by comparing the size of the skeletons to the person in the picture. Ask: **What do you think one of the main body features of this Deinocheirus was?** (Its arms and claws) Show the two cards illustrating the Tyrannosaurus. **What are the two main body features of the Tyrannosaurus shown on these cards?** (Its tail and its jaws) **What can you tell me about the Ultrasaurus from looking at this picture?** (It was gigantic!)

👤 Responding To Individual Needs

Visual Activity Have children trace the individual bones on Poster Book page C6 and match the tracings to the appropriate parts of the dinosaurs.

C10: Arms and Claws of
    Deinocheirus
C11: Skeleton of Tyrannosaurus
C12: Leg Bones of Ultrasaurus
C13: Jaws of Tyrannosaurus

Close

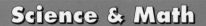

- Ask: **How did you decide which bones belonged to which dinosaurs?** (Have children summarize what they knew from observing the drawings of the dinosaurs and how they inferred from the size and shape of each bone where it belonged.)
- **Extend the Activity** Have children speculate about how scientists would know whether newly found bones belong to a known dinosaur or to one that had never been found before. In the **multi-age classroom**, you may wish to have some children write a story about finding some unknown dinosaur bones and drawing a picture of what they think the dinosaur looked like. Have them share their stories and drawings with the class.

Assess CONCEPT DEVELOPMENT

 Concept Checklist, Assessment Guide p. C76

Use the Concept Checklist to record children's understanding.

- Do children understand that they were modeling scientific behavior?
- Do children recognize that dinosaur skeletons are built from fossil remains?
- Do children understand that dinosaurs have different types and sizes of skeletons?

 Lesson Assessment, Assessment Guide p. C53

Use the Lesson 6 Assessment to evaluate children's understanding of the lesson concept.

 Interview

Scientists often have help from people who do not know how to dig for remains. Have a child explain how to dig up fossils to several "helpers," giving reasons for each instruction. Encourage the helpers to ask questions.

 In My Opinion

Anatomy is the study of animal skeletons and bodies. Have children tell why knowing the anatomy of some dinosaurs would be useful to a scientist. (Children might mention that knowing what a dinosaur looked like can help a scientist learn how it lived.)

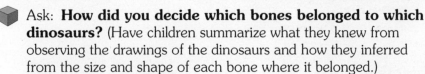

Science & Math

MEASURING BONES Have children refer to the life-size drawings of the bones they recorded on *Science Notebook* page C22. Ask them to measure the length and width of each bone and record the measurements on the drawing.

Science & Language Arts

WRITING ABOUT BONES Have children refer to the life-size drawings of the bones they recorded on *Science Notebook* page C22. Direct them to write a paragraph that describes the bones, including the number of bones found, their shape and size, where in the tray they were found, and from what kind of animals they think the bones came.

INVESTIGATE FURTHER

In the Science Center

Modeling Scientific Behavior

Objective
- **Model** scientific behavior by digging up buried remains.

Process Skill
- **Observe** that all buried remains have been dug up.

Pacing: 20 minutes

Grouping: Small groups of 3–4

Materials
- Activity Card C6
- Goggles
- Newspapers
- Tray of sand and bones that were buried
- Plastic spoons
- Large paper plates
- Variety of small objects (button, piece of chalk, paper clip, eraser)

Procedure
- Have each group rebury the bones they found in the tray of sand. In addition, they should secretly choose two or three other small objects to bury.
- Direct the groups to exchange trays and search for the bones and other buried objects, *observing* carefully that they had found everything. Tell the children to record what they find on a sheet of paper.
- Groups should exchange recording sheets to verify that all buried objects had been found.

Make a FINAL ASSESSMENT

 Review the *Science Notebook*

Ask questions to see if children understand that an animal's size is related to the size of its bones.

 Return to Baseline Assessment

Display the responses to the Assess Prior Knowledge questions and read them aloud. Allow children to make changes and add information learned in the lesson.

 Discussion Starters

Explain to children that paleontologists are scientists who find and dig up dinosaur bones, as well as other kinds of fossil bones. Encourage discussion of the difficulties of finding dinosaur remains, moving them, and figuring out how the bones fit together.

 Role Playing

Ask children to imagine they are scientists digging for fossil bones. Allow children to choose roles as scientists, helpers, or even reporters. Have them role play a situation such as: they have found a completely new dinosaur or they are trying to save buried fossils from a steadily rising flood.

Have children save their work for the portfolio selection process at the end of the unit.

Home-School Connection

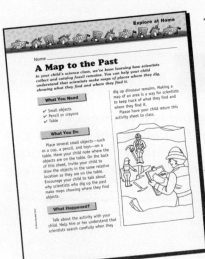

The Explore at Home activity "A Map to the Past" (Teacher Resource Book page C9) invites children to draw a picture, showing the location of objects on a table. After children have done the activity with their families and have returned their activity sheets, invite children to share their drawings with the class.

Science & Art

DRAWING REMAINS

Display the pages at the end of *How Big Were the Dinosaurs?* showing all the dinosaurs in the book. Invite each child to pick a dinosaur and draw what its remains might have looked like. Have the children draw the skulls. Allow them to use straight lines to indicate other bones. Label the remains and display the drawings on the bulletin board.

Looking Ahead

Now that children have learned that fossil bones give clues about dinosaurs' sizes and shapes, they will learn that dinosaurs have different kinds of teeth.

LESSON 7

Investigating

KINDS OF TEETH

In the **LAST LESSON** children learned that fossil bones give clues about the size and shape of animals that lived long ago.

In this **LESSON** children learn what teeth reveal about a dinosaur.

In the **NEXT LESSON** children will learn about dinosaur skeletons.

Resources

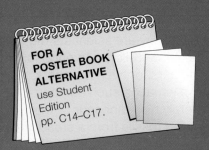

FOR A POSTER BOOK ALTERNATIVE use Student Edition pp. C14–C17.

POSTER BOOK p. C7 AND PICTURE CARDS C14, C15

ACTIVITY CARD C7

TRADE BOOK *How Big Were the Dinosaurs?*

Pacing Guide	
Trade Book	15 minutes
Activity Card	20 minutes
Poster Book & Picture Cards	20 minutes

Teacher Resource Book
• *Home-School Connection*
• *Science Notebook*
• *Activity Support*
• *Assessment Guide*
• *Unit Project Pages*

Equipment Kit

Lesson Overview

Science Theme: Models
Children use **models** of teeth to learn how the shapes of teeth fit their uses. They experiment with the models by using them to tear and grind different kinds of food.

Project 2061 Benchmarks
• Animals eat plants or other animals for food and may also use plants (or even other animals) for shelter and nesting.
• A model of something is different from the real thing but can be used to learn something about the real thing.

Concept
• Flat teeth are good for grinding food, and pointed teeth are good for tearing food.

Objectives
• **Compare** the shapes of teeth that are good for grinding plant matter with teeth that are good for tearing meat.
• **Conclude** that dinosaur teeth give us clues to what they ate.

Science Words
crush	grind	skull
flat teeth	pointed teeth	tear

Activity 🖐 Previewing **Activity Card C7**

Children try to grind two different kinds of food using two different shapes of teeth and generalize that flat teeth are good for grinding food and pointed teeth are good for tearing food.

Grouping
Small groups of 3–4

Materials
• Activity Card C7
• Goggles*
• 2 tree leaves
• 2 golf tees*
• *Science Notebook* p. C23
• 2 small blocks of wood*
• Timer*
• Dry cereal

Advance Preparation
Collect two tree leaves (or two plant leaves) for each group.

For Best Results
Have children cover the work surface with newspapers to facilitate clean up of any spilled cereal or leaf matter.

* In Equipment Kit

Science Background

Plant-eating dinosaurs had strong jaw muscles that moved forward and backward. Some plant eaters had many teeth and ate very coarse plants. New teeth replaced old, worn teeth. Other plant eaters with no grinding teeth used peg- or spoon-shaped front teeth to strip leaves from branches. They swallowed these whole and ground them up in a part of the stomach similar to a chicken's gizzard. Plant eaters with small, weak teeth could eat only soft plants.

Meat-eating dinosaurs usually had powerful jaws with a special joint to hold prey. They used daggerlike teeth to slice off chunks of meat. Some teeth were serrated like steak knives. Meat eaters needed no chewing teeth because they swallowed the meat chunks whole.

Real World Connection Animals today have flat or pointed teeth suited to what they eat, just as the dinosaurs did.

▲ Marshosaurus

Books for Children

Dinosaurs by Eugene S. Gaffney (Golden Press/Western Publishing Company, Inc., 1990). Contains information on various dinosaurs. For more advanced students, or for the teacher to read aloud. (Grade 3 and up)

Dinosaurs by Encyclopedia Britannica (Publications International, Ltd., 1993). Various tidbits about the dinosaurs are presented in an interesting style that is concise and that will catch children's attention. (Grades 2–5)

The New Illustrated Dinosaur Dictionary by Helen Roney L. Sattler (Beech Tree Books, 1990). A dictionary with entries for all known dinosaurs and other animals of the Mesozoic Era, as well as general topics relating to dinosaurs. Read aloud for information and share the illustrations. (Grades 2–5)

Setting the Stage

Stage

Setting the Stage

Using the Trade Book

Read aloud the pages about Tyrannosaurus rex, Allosaurus, and Torvosaurus in *How Big Were the Dinosaurs?* Ask children what Tyrannosaurus, Allosaurus, and Torvosaurus ate. (Meat) Have children describe the shape of the dinosaur teeth. (Long and pointed) ⬛ Ask: **How did meat eaters use their sharp teeth?** (Help children conclude that they cut or tore out chunks of meat to eat.) Then ask what dinosaurs ate if they didn't eat meat. (If children do not recall that other dinosaurs ate plant material, read the pages about Triceratops, Hypselosaurus, and Supersaurus.) ⬛ Promote discussion by asking: **What kind of teeth do you think plant eaters would need to grind up leaves and branches?** (Children may respond that they would not need long, sharp teeth like the meat eaters but, rather, flat teeth that are good for nipping, chopping, and grinding plant matter.)

How Big Were the Dinosaurs?
by Bernard Most

Activity 🖐 Assess Prior Knowledge

Making a Baseline Assessment
Ask: **What did the dinosaurs eat? Did all dinosaurs have the same shape of teeth? Could a dinosaur eat plants easily if its teeth were sharp? What shape of teeth would a meat eater need? How can you tell what a dinosaur ate?** Record responses on chart paper and save them for comparison in Make a Final Assessment at the end of the lesson.

Using the
ACTIVITY CARD

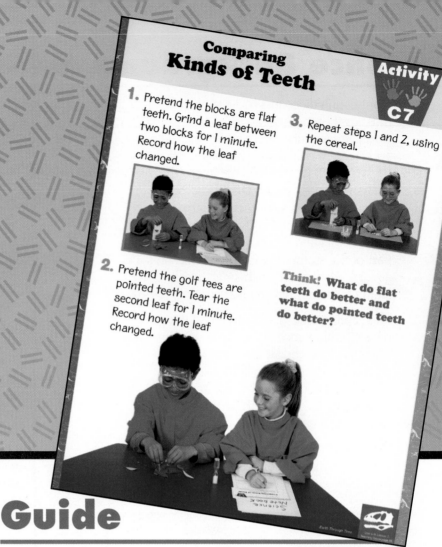

Organize

Objectives

- **Compare** the shapes of teeth that are good for grinding plant matter with teeth that are good for tearing meat.
- **Conclude** that dinosaur teeth give us clues to what they ate.

Process Skills

- **Use models** of teeth to predict which shape works better to grind food and which shape works better to tear food.
- **Experiment** to discover which tooth shape works better to grind food and which tooth shape will work better to tear food.
- **Predict** which models of teeth will grind or tear food better.

Pacing: 20 minutes

Grouping: Small groups of 3–4

Materials

- Activity Card C7
- Goggles
- 2 tree leaves
- 2 golf tees
- *Science Notebook* p. C23
- 2 small blocks of wood
- Timer
- Dry cereal

Safety: Instruct children to wear goggles, not to put the golf tees, leaves, or cereal in their mouths, and not to misuse the materials.

Guide

- **Warm-Up** Ask children to feel their teeth with their tongues and note the difference between the front and back teeth. Encourage children to describe how they use each kind of tooth to eat food. Display the small blocks of wood and the golf tees and have children discuss which of their teeth are like each object. Have them *predict* which model of teeth will **grind** food better and which model will **tear** food better.
- In step 1, have children *experiment* for one minute, grinding the leaf with the blocks. *(use models)* Make sure that they understand to use the flat sides of the blocks to grind and not the pointed corners. Then have them draw in their *Science Notebooks* what the leaf looks like.
- In step 2, have children *experiment* for one minute, tearing the leaf with the golf tees. *(use models)* After drawing in their *Science Notebooks* what the leaf looks like, have children compare the two drawings.
- In step 3, repeat steps 1 and 2, using cereal. *(use models)*
- Discuss whether children's predictions were borne out by their experiments. They should have observed that the small blocks were good for grinding food and the golf tees were good for tearing food.
- Ask: **How do you use your front teeth to eat food?** (To bite, or chop and tear) **How do you use your back teeth?** (To chew, or **crush** and grind) **How are your front and back teeth different?** (Front: more **pointed teeth**; back: **flat teeth**) Explain that teeth are rooted in the jaw, which is part of the **skull** or skeleton of the head.

Responding To Individual Needs

Inclusive Activity Have children use the golf tees and small blocks to try to tear up a piece of lunch meat. Ask them to identify which model of teeth worked better and tell why. (Golf tees; they were pointed and sharp and could tear the lunch meat better.)

Name_____

Comparing Kinds of Teeth

How the Leaf Changed

Grinding With Blocks	Tearing With Golf Tees

How the Cereal Changed

Grinding With Blocks	Tearing With Golf Tees

What do flat teeth do better and what do pointed teeth do better?

_____

Close

- Ask: **If a dinosaur's teeth were sharp or pointed, what do you think it ate?** (Meat) **What do you think it ate if its teeth were flat?** (Plants)
- **Think!** Answer: Help children to infer that flat teeth grind better and pointed teeth tear better.
- **Extend the Activity** Have children describe which teeth would work better to bite off and then chew up corn on the cob, peas, and barbecue ribs. In the **multi-age classroom**, you may wish to have some children make drawings of their teeth and to label what each tooth does best.

Assess
PERFORMANCE

 Expected Results

- Did children use blocks and golf tees to try to grind and tear the leaves and the cereal?
- Did children make drawings of the leaves and decide which model of teeth worked better for grinding food?
- Did children make drawings of the cereal and decide which model of teeth worked better for tearing food?

 Process Skills Checklist, Assessment Guide p. C68

Use the Process Skills Checklist to record children's performance.

- Did children *use models* of teeth to *predict* which shapes work better to grind food and which shapes work better to tear food?
- Did children *experiment* to find out whether their predictions were correct?

Group Skills Checklist, Assessment Guide p. C69

Use the Group Skills Checklist to record children's performance.

- Did children *take initiative* to begin the activity?
- Did they *discuss* which teeth were better for biting and which were better for chewing?

Alternate **Activity** USES DIFFERENT MATERIALS

Pacing: 10 minutes
Grouping: Individual
Materials

- Crackers (any kind)

Procedure

- Have each child eat a cracker. Direct children to pay attention to how they use their teeth to eat the cracker. Ask them to describe which teeth they used to take a bite and which they used to chew or grind the cracker.

Discuss the shapes of children's front teeth and back teeth.

Ask: **What kind of food does each tooth shape help you to eat? Tell how.** (The sharper teeth are good for

biting, tearing, and cutting food; the flatter teeth are good for grinding and pulverizing food.) Help children record their answers on a chart. If they have difficulty thinking of foods, have them visualize the shapes of different animals' teeth and what they eat. You may wish to have children use copies of the Activity Support blackline master titled "Chart/Survey" (Teacher Resource Book page C34) to record their answers.

Using the POSTER BOOK & PICTURE CARDS

How are the teeth of these dinosaurs different?
What do you think each dinosaur is going to eat?
Tell how their teeth help them eat certain foods.

POSTER BOOK PAGE

Earth Through Time C7

Organize

Objectives

- **Compare** the shapes of teeth that are good for grinding plant matter with teeth that are good for tearing meat.
- **Conclude** that dinosaur teeth give us clues to what they ate.

Process Skill

- **Observe** what dinosaurs ate and how their teeth, skulls, and jaws differed.

Pacing: 20 minutes

Grouping: Whole class

Materials

- Poster Book p. C7 with overlay
- Picture Cards C14, C15
  (See backs of Picture Cards for questions, facts, and related activities.)
- Erasable marker

For Best Results: If you use an erasable marker on the Poster Book page, wipe it off immediately after the lesson.

Using the Student Edition: You may wish to use Student Edition pages C14–C17 to extend or replace the Poster Book lesson.

Guide

❶ Edmontosaurus (ed mänt ə sôr′əs)
❷ Albertosaurus (al bʉrt ə sôr′əs)
❸ Lizard

- **Warm-Up** Remind children that some dinosaurs were plant eaters and others were meat eaters. Discuss examples of meat-eating and plant-eating animals alive today, such as lions, cows, and horses.
- **Poster Book** Display the Poster Book page C7 without the overlay. Have children *observe* and compare the shapes of the heads and jaws of both dinosaurs. Ask: **How would you describe the teeth of the dinosaur in the front?** (Pointed, sharp, big) **Why do you think you can't see the teeth of the second dinosaur?** (Too far back in its mouth)
- Now pull down the overlay. Ask: **How would you describe the teeth of the dinosaur at the top of the poster?** (Set back in jaw, flat, smaller) **What do you think each dinosaur is going to eat?** Have volunteers use the erasable marker to draw a line from each dinosaur to what they think the dinosaur is going to eat. (Front dinosaur: lizard; back dinosaur: plant)
- Help children recognize that meat-eating dinosaurs needed sharp pointed teeth to tear meat, while plant-eating dinosaurs needed flat, blunt teeth to chop and grind plant material.
- **Picture Cards** Have children examine the Picture Cards—C14: Triceratops and C15: Allosaurus. Ask them whether they think each dinosaur was a plant eater or a meat eater. (Triceratops had flat teeth good for grinding food; Allosaurus had pointed teeth good for tearing meat.)

Responding To Individual Needs

Children Acquiring English Proficiency   Have children draw the two kinds of dinosaur teeth shown on the Picture Cards. Ask them to label the two shapes (pointed; flat) both in English and in their native language. Display the drawings for the entire class to view. Encourage all children to pronounce the words in both languages.

How are the teeth of these dinosaurs different?
What do you think each dinosaur is going to eat?
Tell how their teeth help them eat certain foods.

Earth Through Time C7

Close

- **Why are the teeth of plant-eating dinosaurs flat?** (Flat teeth are better suited to nipping off and grinding plant matter.)
- **Extend the Activity** Discuss what humans do to help them eat meat since their teeth are not as sharp as those of other meat-eating animals. (Cooking or pounding meat to soften it, using chemical meat tenderizers, or using a knife and fork to cut the meat into smaller pieces)

Assess
CONCEPT DEVELOPMENT

 Concept Checklist, Assessment Guide p. C77

Use the Concept Checklist to record children's understanding.

- Do children recognize that flat teeth are good for grinding food and pointed teeth are good for tearing food?
- Do children understand that scientists can tell what a dinosaur ate by looking at its teeth?

 Lesson Assessment, Assessment Guide p. C54

Use the Lesson 7 Assessment to evaluate children's understanding of the lesson concept.

 Make a Concept Map

As a class, make a concept map that lists various plant foods, such as bananas or hay, and the names of animals alive today that eat these foods. Then do the same with animal foods and animals that eat them. Include on the concept map the shapes of the teeth of the animals named.

 Role-Playing

Have individual children play the parts of a horse, a chimpanzee, a cow, a lion, and other animals. They should show how they move their jaws to eat. Then have them explain what the animals are eating and what their teeth look like.

Science & Art

SCULPTING TEETH

Have children make clay models of dinosaur teeth. Allow them to look at the pictures of the teeth on Poster Book page C7 and other sources. Help children to label their sculptures and to arrange a Dinosaur Teeth display.

Science & Language Arts

USING WORDS

Let children use their imagination to write a paragraph about why they would like to be a plant-eating or a meat-eating dinosaur. Have them explain what kind of teeth they would need to survive and describe the kind of food they would need to find to eat. Before they write their paragraphs, you may wish to have children use copies of the Activity Support blackline master titled "Word Web" (Teacher Resource Book page C32).

INVESTIGATE FURTHER

UNIT PROJECT LINK

Dinosaur Place: Adding Environment

Have children draw on the Unit Project page the teeth of a plant-eating dinosaur and a meat-eating dinosaur. Then have children draw arrows to match each dinosaur with the kind of food it might have eaten.

Encourage children to draw on construction paper the outlines of foods that plant-eating dinosaurs and meat-eating dinosaurs might have eaten. Have children cut out and mount the food outlines near the outlines of the dinosaurs that might have eaten them. Invite children to also make other environmental outlines such as trees, volcanoes, and water to mount or hang around the room.

Use Unit Project page C100 in the Teacher Resource Book with this activity.

In the Science Center

Relating Teeth to What Dinosaurs Ate

Objective
- **Conclude** that dinosaur teeth give us clues to what they ate.

Process Skill
- **Infer** what a dinosaur ate by looking at its teeth.

Pacing: 10 minutes

Grouping: Pairs

Materials
- Picture Cards C1, C2, C5, C9, C14, C15

Procedure
- Direct one child to choose a Picture Card and hold a hand over the picture of the dinosaur so that only the teeth show. The other child should look at the teeth and decide whether the dinosaur ate meat or plants. Have the child explain how he or she could tell what the dinosaur ate. (By looking at the shape of the teeth) *(infer)*
- Have children repeat the procedure, taking turns choosing a Picture Card.

Make a FINAL ASSESSMENT

 Review the *Science Notebook*

Ask children to describe what kind of teeth work best for eating meats or for eating plants and why.

 Return to Baseline Assessment

Display children's responses to the Assess Prior Knowledge questions about dinosaurs' teeth and their shapes. Read the responses and ask if children want to make changes or add information learned in the lesson.

 In My Opinion

Ask children to describe what would happen if a plant eater tried to eat a small animal. Then have them do the same with a meat eater and a branch of a tree. Encourage them to use their imaginations.

 Writing

Ask children to imagine they are restaurant managers and write menus with items for plant-eating dinosaurs and for meat-eating dinosaurs. Encourage them to use the names of other dinosaurs when planning dinners for meat-eating dinosaurs. They may use the names of today's plants in the dinners for the plant eaters.

Have children save their work for the portfolio selection process at the end of the unit.

Home-School Connection

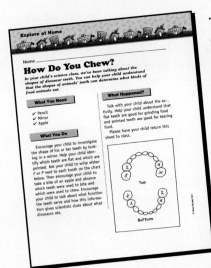

The Explore at Home activity "How Do You Chew?" (Teacher Resource Book page C10) invites children to investigate the shape of their teeth and to explore how they bite and chew an apple. After children have done the activity with their families and have returned their activity sheets, invite children to share their discoveries with the class.

Science & Language Arts

WRITING A LETTER Children should use their imaginations as they write a letter to a veterinarian explaining that their pet dinosaur has a broken tooth that must be taken care of soon. They should explain why the dinosaur needs its tooth fixed and what will happen if it is not fixed soon.

Looking Ahead

Now that children have learned that different shapes of teeth are needed to eat plants and animals, they will learn how to tell the shape of a dinosaur from its skeleton.

LESSON 8

Investigating

DINOSAUR SKELETONS

In the **LAST LESSON** children learned what teeth reveal about a dinosaur.

In this **LESSON** children learn about dinosaur skeletons.

In the **NEXT LESSON** children will learn that dinosaurs had some things in common with today's animals.

Resources

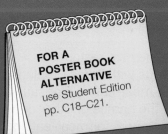

POSTER BOOK p. C8

FOR A **POSTER BOOK ALTERNATIVE** use Student Edition pp. C18–C21.

ACTIVITY CARD C8

TRADE BOOK *How Big Were the Dinosaurs?*

Pacing Guide	
Trade Book	15 minutes
Activity Card	20 minutes
Poster Book	20 minutes

Teacher Resource Book
- *Home-School Connection*
- *Science Notebook*
- *Activity Support*
- *Assessment Guide*
- *Unit Project Pages*

Audiotape or CD

Equipment Kit

Lesson Overview

Science Theme: Models

Children put together and examine **models** of dinosaur skeletons. In these activities, they observe that they can tell about a dinosaur's size and shape by examining its skeleton.

Project 2061 Benchmark

- Some kinds of organisms that once lived on earth have completely disappeared, although they were something like others that are alive today.

Concept

- Skeletons are clues to sizes and shapes of dinosaurs.

Objectives

- **Assemble** a dinosaur skeleton.
- **Infer** the shape of a dinosaur from its skeleton.

Science Words

skeleton
Chasmosaurus (kaz mō sôr′əs)
Euoplocephalus (yoo ō plə sef′ə ləs)

Activity  Previewing Activity Card C8

As children tape together paper pieces of dinosaur bones to make a skeleton, they generalize that scientists can tell the size and shape of a dinosaur by looking at its skeleton.

Grouping

Small groups of 3–4

Materials

- Activity Card C8
- Activity Support blackline masters: Dinosaur Skeleton 1 (Chasmosaurus Skeleton), Dinosaur Skeleton 2 (Euoplocephalus Skeleton)
- Crayons or colored pencils
- Tape
- *Science Notebook* p. C24

Advance Preparation

Make enough copies of both Activity Support blackline masters to give each group one complete dinosaur skeleton for the Activity Card and one for later. You might ask an upper-grade child to assist in cutting out the bones. Make sure the bones of each dinosaur skeleton are kept together.

For Best Results

Glue the skeleton pieces on tagboard or index cards before cutting them out, so they will be easier for the children to use. Don't let children see the blackline master pictures of the dinosaurs.

*In Equipment Kit

Science Background

In the laboratory, scientists use tiny picks and air jacks to remove any rock material from fossil bones. They reinforce the bones by painting them or injecting them with modern materials to strengthen them.

Dinosaur fossils can be recognized by their pelvic bones with open hip sockets. According to the shape of the bones, dinosaurs are classified as Ornithischia (bird-hipped) or Saurischia (reptile-hipped).

Dinosaurs have strong, straight ankle joints directly under their bodies so their limbs can stand upright. The bones often have marks showing where muscles and ligaments may have been attached. This helps scientists learn how the dinosaur moved.

THESCELOSAURUS NEGLECTUS

▲ Bird-hipped Thescelosaurus

Books for Children

***The Dinosaur Question and Answer Book* by Sylvia Funston (Little, Brown and Company, 1992).** The most commonly desired information about dinosaurs and the time they lived is presented in question-and-answer format. For use with advanced students, or as a read-aloud. Use to stimulate discussion. (Grades 4–7)

***Dinosaurium* by Barbara Brenner (Bantam Books, 1993).** Describes a museum tour through the Triassic, Jurassic, and Cretaceous Periods, with information about the names and habitats of the dinosaurs. Includes questions for the reader to answer. (PreK– Grade 3)

***The Illustrated Encyclopedia of Dinosaurs* by David Norman (Random House, 1985).** A detailed examination of the world of dinosaurs, their appearance, behavior, and families. This book also describes current theories about their extinction. In addition, an explanation of how paleontologists study fossil remains is given. Use with more advanced students, or read aloud. (Grades 3–5)

Setting the Stage

• • • • • • • • • • • •

Using the Trade Book

Invite children to feel their leg and arm bones. Have them bend their knees and elbows and try to bend their legs and arms backward. Let them find out how their skeletons let them move and what movements are impossible. Explain that the way the bones fit together determines how an animal can move.

Display the dinosaur pictures at the end of *How Big Were the Dinosaurs?* Ask children to decide which dinosaurs had skeletons that let them walk on two legs. Ask: **Which dinosaurs had unusual skulls?** (Children might mention Triceratops, Parasaurolophus, and Ankylosaurus.)

🟦 Display the arms and claws of Deinocheirus and the claws of Therizinosaurus together with Picture Card C10 titled Arms and Claws of Deinocheirus. Ask: **Why don't we know more about the sizes of Deinocheirus and Therizinosaurus?** (There have not been enough bones from these dinosaurs found to allow scientists to figure out their size and shape.)

Activity ✋ Assess Prior Knowledge

Making a Baseline Assessment
Ask: **What is the skeleton of an animal? How are all dinosaur skeletons alike? How does a dinosaur's skeleton show its size and shape?** Record responses on chart paper and save them for comparison in Make a Final Assessment at the end of the lesson.

Using Technology

Audiotape or CD: *Grade 2 Science Songs*
After completing Activity Card C8, play the song "Dinosaur Tango" for the class. Help children make up additional verses to describe other dinosaurs.

Using the
ACTIVITY CARD

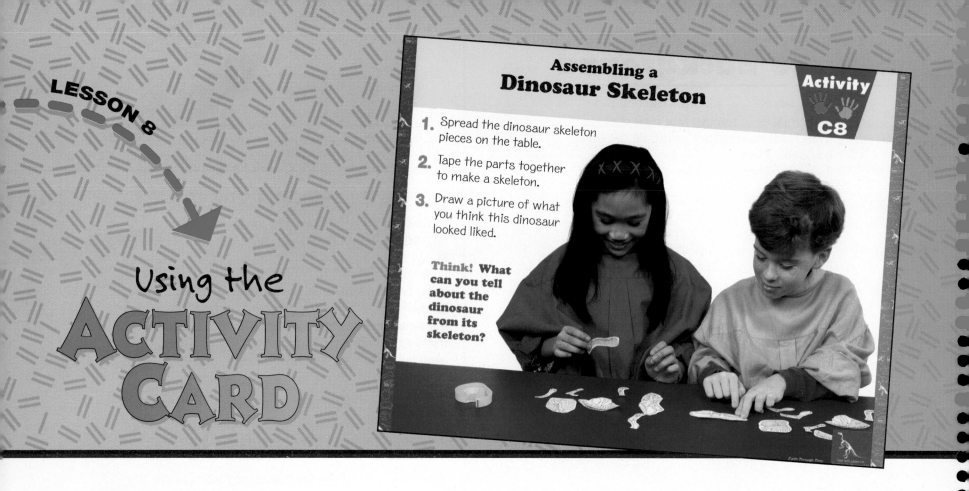

Assembling a Dinosaur Skeleton

Activity C8

1. Spread the dinosaur skeleton pieces on the table.
2. Tape the parts together to make a skeleton.
3. Draw a picture of what you think this dinosaur looked liked.

Think! What can you tell about the dinosaur from its skeleton?

Organize

Objectives

- **Assemble** a dinosaur skeleton.
- **Infer** the shape of a dinosaur from its skeleton.

Process Skills

- **Observe** how the bones of a dinosaur skeleton fit together.
- **Make** and **use a model** of a dinosaur skeleton by assembling paper skeleton pieces.
- **Infer** the shape of the dinosaur from its skeleton.

Pacing: 20 minutes

Grouping: Small groups of 3–4

Materials
- Activity Card C8
- Dinosaur skeleton pieces
- Tape
- *Science Notebook* p. C24

Safety: Instruct children to be careful when handling the paper skeleton pieces so that they do not get paper cuts.

Guide

- **Warm-Up** Ask children to hold out one hand, fingers spread. Have them use their other hand to feel the bones in their fingers and hand. Lead them to describe where the bones are in their hands. Point out that all the bones in their body make up their **skeleton.**

- In step 1, give each group Dinosaur Skeleton 1 pieces or Dinosaur Skeleton 2 pieces. Have children spread the dinosaur skeleton pieces on the table. Ask questions to help them identify the skull, hip socket, and other bones. Help them compare the long limb bones with their own arm and leg bones. *(use a model)*

- In step 2, allow time for children to move the skeleton pieces around to observe where each fits best. When they are satisfied with the arrangement, instruct them to tape together, or assemble, the skeleton. *(make a model)*

- As children do step 3, help them infer the shape of the dinosaur from the assembled skeleton. Children should draw in their *Science Notebooks* what they think the dinosaur looked like.

Responding To Individual Needs

Inclusive Activity Prepare outlines of the two dinosaurs from completed skeletons. Give children the outlines of the two dinosaurs. Help them place the bones within the outlines to figure out which dinosaur skeleton they have and how the bones fit together. In the **multi-age classroom**, you may wish to have some children help other children place the bones in the outlines.

 Expected Results

- Did children make a skeleton by taping together the bones that fit together?
- Did they use the assembled skeleton to make a drawing of the dinosaur?

 Process Skills Checklist, Assessment Guide p. C68

Use the Process Skills Checklist to record children's performance.

- Did children *observe* how the dinosaur bones fit together?
- Did children *make a model* of a dinosaur skeleton by correctly assembling paper skeleton pieces?
- Did children *infer* the shape of a dinosaur from its skeleton?

 Group Skills Checklist, Assessment Guide p. C69

Use the Group Skills Checklist to record children's performance.

- Did children *encourage* each other to participate in the activity?
- Did they *share* the tasks of the activity?
- Did they *communicate clearly* what they could tell about a dinosaur from its skeleton?

Close

- Tell children the name of each dinosaur and its actual length. (**Chasmosaurus**: 17 ft, **Euoplocephalus**: 20 ft) Ask: **Which bones helped you the most in figuring out the dinosaur's shape?** (Children might mention the skull and other one-of-a-kind bones.)
- **Think!** Answer: A dinosaur skeleton gives clues to the dinosaur's shape, size, kind and number of feet.
- **Extend the Activity** Have children with the same dinosaur skeletons compare their drawings. Then give each group the other dinosaur's skeleton pieces and repeat the activity. In the **multi-age classroom**, you may wish to combine and mix up the skeleton pieces of the two dinosaurs and have some of the children try to complete the two skeletons.

Alternate Activity 👋 USES LESS TIME

Pacing: 10 minutes
Grouping: Individual
Materials

- Dinosaur skeleton pieces
- Glue
- Crayons or colored pencils
- Paper

Procedure

- Give each child all the skeleton pieces for one dinosaur. Have children decide how the bones fit together to form a complete skeleton.

- Tell children to glue the assembled skeleton onto a sheet of paper and then draw an outline of the dinosaur around the skeleton. In the **multi-age classroom**, you may wish to have some children help other children glue their assembled skeletons. 🔲 Discuss with children the shapes of the dinosaurs. Ask: **What can you tell about a dinosaur from its skeleton?** (Its shape, size, number of legs)

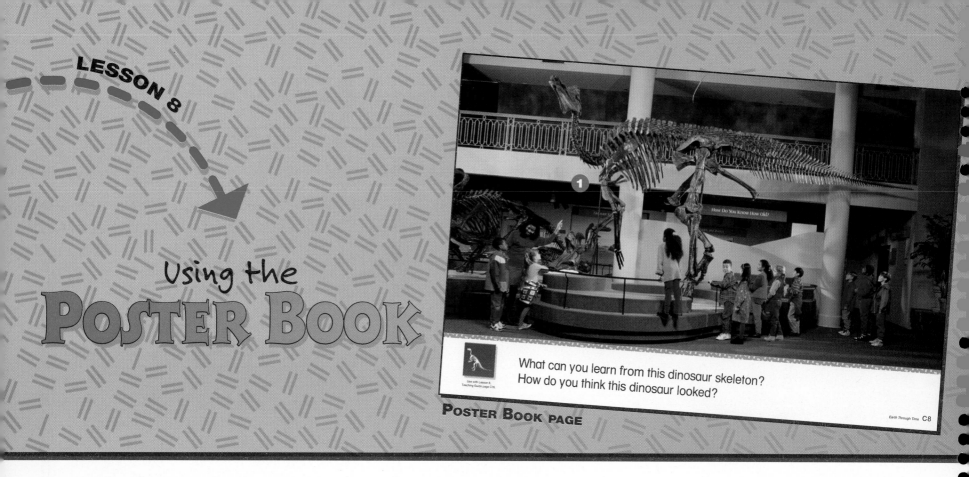

Using the
POSTER BOOK

What can you learn from this dinosaur skeleton?
How do you think this dinosaur looked?

POSTER BOOK PAGE

Earth Through Time C8

Organize

Objective

- **Infer** the shape of a dinosaur from its skeleton.

Process Skill

- **Observe** a dinosaur skeleton for clues to its shape.

Pacing: 20 minutes

Grouping: Whole class

Materials

- Poster Book p. C8 with overlay
- Erasable marker

For Best Results: If you use an erasable marker on the Poster Book page, wipe it off immediately after the lesson.

Using the Student Edition: You may wish to use Student Edition pages C18–C21 to extend or replace the Poster Book lesson.

Guide

① Corythosaurus (kôr inth ə sôr'əs) skeleton

- **Warm-Up** Review with children that when dinosaur skeletons are found, the bones are all mixed up or some, even many, can be missing. Explain that for scientists, assembling a dinosaur skeleton can be like doing a jigsaw puzzle with missing pieces.
- **Poster Book** Display the picture of the Corythosaurus skeleton without the overlay. Ask children to identify various bones. Have them count the number of fingers on the front claws.
- Ask: **What part of this dinosaur looks very different from the same part of other dinosaurs?** (The skull with a crest on it) After children identify the crest on the skull, have them speculate on its purpose. (Children may suggest it's there to frighten other dinosaurs, to protect their heads, to look good, or to help make sounds.)
- Ask: **What animals that are alive today have things on their heads that help us identify the animals?** (Roosters, elephants, deer, bulls)
- Ask volunteers to use an erasable marker to draw on the Poster Book page the outline of the dinosaur's body around parts of the skeleton. Outlines should indicate that children inferred the shape of the dinosaur from the shape of its skeleton. Guide children who have difficulty making the outline. Explain that they can follow the large curves of the skeleton to see how the dinosaur might have looked. *(observe)* Then pull down the overlay to show children an artist's drawing of a Corythosaurus.

🌐 Responding To Individual Needs

Gifted and Talented Children   Have children compare the skeleton of the dinosaur with their own skeleton and identify similarities and differences in posture, number of fingers or toes, and other characteristics. You may wish to have them describe what they discovered orally and tape-record their responses.

What can you learn from this dinosaur skeleton?
How do you think this dinosaur looked?

Earth Through Time C8

POSTER BOOK PAGE WITH OVERLAY

Close

- With the overlay down on the Poster Book page, have children observe how the dinosaur's shape follows the outline of its skeleton. Discuss with children that the overlay is a combination of how some scientists and the artist think this dinosaur might have looked.
- Ask: **What do you know about a dinosaur from its skeleton?** (Its size and general shape)
- **Extend the Activity** Have children compare their outline of the dinosaur with the shape on the overlay.

 Concept Checklist, Assessment Guide p. C78

Use the Concept Checklist to record children's understanding.

- Do children recognize that different dinosaurs have differently shaped skeletons?
- Do children understand that dinosaur skeletons are clues to the sizes and shapes of the dinosaurs?

 Lesson Assessment, Assessment Guide p. C55

Use the Lesson 8 Assessment to evaluate children's understanding of the lesson concept.

 Group Discussion

Invite children to imagine that they are scientists who have discovered dinosaur bones. Ask: **How would you know how big the dinosaur was?** (Scientists must figure out what each bone is and how the bones fit together, then determine the dinosaur's size.)

 Designing

Have each child design a dinosaur skeleton. Children should draw a skull, a neck, a backbone, legs or legs and arms, toes or fingers or claws, and a tail. The skeleton should show whether the dinosaur walks on two or four legs. Then have them draw the outline of the dinosaur.

Science & Math

MEASURING Have children return to their completed dinosaur skeletons from Activity Card C8. Help them to measure out 17 feet (actual length of Chasmosaurus) and 20 feet (actual length of Euoplocephalus) on the floor with tape. Then have children use their model dinosaur skeletons to determine how many times the length of the model dinosaur fits into the actual length of the dinosaur.

Science & Art

MAKING MODELS Ask if any children have been to museums and seen models of dinosaurs on display. Tell them that experts create these models by studying dinosaur skeletons and then building metal frames that resemble the skeletons. They then add other materials to mold the body shape and a covering to represent the dinosaur's skin. Have children experiment with molding their own dinosaurs with clay or aluminum foil.

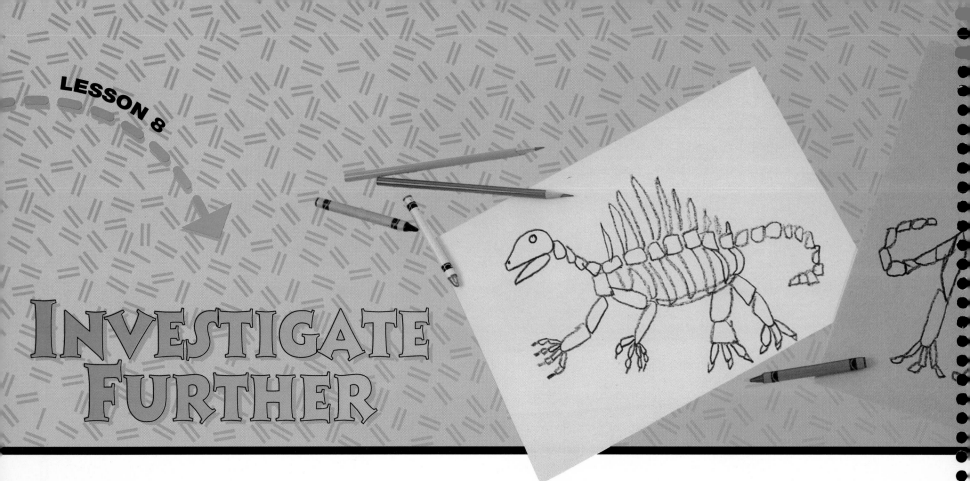

INVESTIGATE FURTHER

In the Science Center

Determining Sizes and Shapes of Bones

Objective
- **Infer** the shape of a dinosaur from its skeleton.

Process Skills
- **Observe** the shapes of a dinosaur's body parts.
- **Infer** the shape of a dinosaur's skeleton from the shape of its body.

Pacing: 20 minutes

Grouping: Pairs

Materials
- Poster Book p. C6
- Crayons
- Paper

Procedure
- Ask each child to choose one dinosaur and *observe* the shape of its skull, neck, legs, feet, and tail. Then have children use their observations to draw the dinosaur's skeleton, showing how the bones fit together.
- Discuss children's drawings and ask them to explain how or why they chose some of the bone shapes. The bones drawn should show that children *inferred* the shape of the skeleton and of individual bones from the shape of the body.

Home-School Connection

The Explore at Home activity "Those Bones" (Teacher Resource Book page C11) invites children to look at pictures of animals and to make animal skeleton models out of pipe cleaners or twist ties. After children have done the activity with their families and have brought in their skeleton models, invite children to share them with the class.

Make a FINAL ASSESSMENT

 Review the *Science Notebook*

Ask questions to see if children know that they can infer a dinosaur's shape from its skeleton.

 Return to Baseline Assessment

Display the responses to the Assess Prior Knowledge questions and read them aloud. Let children change or add information about how to relate dinosaurs' skeletons and shapes.

 Discussion Starters

Ask: **If scientists discovered dinosaur fossil bones, how could they tell if the bones belong to a kind of dinosaur they already know about or to an unknown kind of dinosaur?** (The scientists could assemble the bones and compare them with the skeletons of known dinosaurs.)

 Writing

Display the pages showing all the dinosaurs in *How Big Were the Dinosaurs?* Ask each child to choose a dinosaur and write a description of its skeleton, using this sentence structure: *I know the _____ (bone) is _____ (adjective) because _____ .* Children should show that they understand that the body outline follows the skeleton.

Have children save their work for the portfolio selection process at the end of the unit.

Science & Social Studies

USING A MAP Display a map of the United States. Help children find Utah and Colorado. Tell them that many dinosaur fossils have been found in these states in areas that are very dry. Have children recall what the climate was like when dinosaurs were alive. (Wet and warm) Ask: **What do you think happened to the climate in these states since the time of the dinosaurs?** (It changed.)

Looking Ahead

Now that children have learned to tell the shape of a dinosaur from its skeleton, they will learn that, like the dinosaurs, some animals alive today may become extinct.

LESSON 9

Investigating DINOSAURS AND LIVING ANIMALS

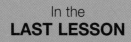

In the **LAST LESSON** children learned about dinosaur skeletons.

In this **LESSON** children learn that dinosaurs had some things in common with today's animals.

Resources

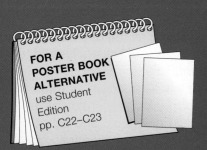

FOR A **POSTER BOOK ALTERNATIVE** use Student Edition pp. C22–C23

POSTER BOOK p. C9 AND PICTURE CARDS C16, C17, C18, C19, C20, C21, C22

ACTIVITY CARD C9

TRADE BOOK *How Big Were the Dinosaurs?*

Pacing Guide

Trade Book	15 minutes
Activity Card	20 minutes
Poster Book & Picture Cards	20 minutes

Teacher Resource Book
• *Home-School Connection*
• *Science Notebook*
• *Activity Support*
• *Assessment Guide*
• *Unit Project Pages*

Videotape

Equipment Kit

Lesson Overview

Science Theme: Constancy and Change
Children compare the body parts of dinosaurs with those of living animals. In these activities, they see **constancy** in the way that living animals resemble dinosaurs and **change** in the ways that today's animals differ from those that lived long ago.

Project 2061 Benchmark
• Some kinds of organisms that once lived on earth have completely disappeared, although they were something like others that are alive today.

Concept
• Although dinosaurs became extinct a long time ago, some of them had characteristics similar to animals that are alive today.

Objectives
• **Compare** dinosaurs with living animals.
• **Conclude** that some animals alive today are in danger of becoming extinct.

Science Words
endangered   extinct

Activity Previewing Activity Card C9

Children match dinosaurs with living animals that have similar traits and generalize that living animals help us learn about dinosaurs.

Grouping
Small groups of 3–4

Materials
• Activity Card C9
• Activity Support blackline masters: Dinosaur Cards, Living-Animal Cards
• *Science Notebook*  p. C25

Advance Preparation
Make enough copies of the Activity Support blackline masters to give both sets of cards to each group. Glue the cards to sturdy index cards, tagboard, or heavy construction paper before cutting them out.

*In Equipment Kit

Pressed for Time?
This lesson targets a key concept in this unit. Use this lesson and Lessons 1, 2, 3, 5 and 6 if your teaching time is limited.

Science Background

Dinosaurs became extinct about 65 million years ago, probably in a catastrophe. There are many theories about what the catastrophe was. It may have been an asteroid that hit the earth and changed the environment so much that dinosaurs could not continue to live. Many other species became extinct at the same time, and there have been other great extinctions through the ages.

Today many animals are in danger of becoming extinct. In 1973, the first successful United States Endangered Species Act was passed. Under the act, federal officials can designate a species as endangered, protect it, and take steps to increase its numbers. This act has helped save the bald eagle.

Books for Children

Evolution by Joanna Cole (Crowell, 1987). Well-presented information on the theory of evolution for a young audience. (Grades K–3)

Living Fossils by Joyce Pope (Steck-Vaughn, 1992). Examines living animals and plants that have managed to survive over millions of years unchanged. Examples include the shark, crocodile, horseshoe crab, dragonfly, and ginko tree. Use with your more advanced students. (Grades 4–8)

The Magic School Bus in the Time of the Dinosaurs by Joanna Cole (Scholastic, 1994). Ms. Frizzle's class goes back in time to the dinosaurs to discover adventure and interesting facts. (Grades 2–5)

If You've Ever Seen a Rhinoceros Charge . . . by Duncan Dobie (Bucksnort Publishing, 1994). Beautiful illustrations introduce children to many animals that have become endangered. (Grades 1–4)

Setting the
Stage

Using the Trade Book

Turn to the dinosaur pictures at the end of *How Big Were the Dinosaurs?* Have children identify dinosaurs that resemble living animals. ■ Ask: **Which living animals have long necks like Ultrasaurus?** (Giraffes, swans, ostriches) **Long tails?** (Squirrels, crocodiles, rats) **Sharp claws?** (Roosters, cats, monkeys) **Big, thick legs?** (Elephants, rhinoceroses, hippopotamuses) **Heads like Shantungosaurus?** (Ducks) **Plates on their bodies?** (Alligators, crocodiles, lizards) **Horns?** (Deer, bulls)

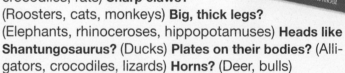

■ **What might cause some kinds of animals to die out?** (They might be eaten or might not find enough food.) **How might humans put some kinds of animals in danger of dying out?** (They can kill animals or change the environment so there is no food or shelter.) **How can humans help prevent some animals from dying out?** (Have children relate anything they know about how humans are protecting some animals.)

Activity  Assess Prior Knowledge

Making a Baseline Assessment
Ask: **What living animals look somewhat like dinosaurs? What can they tell us about dinosaurs? What animals are in danger of disappearing today? How do humans help, cause, or prevent this?** Record responses on chart paper and save them for comparison in Make a Final Assessment at the end of the lesson.

Using Technology

Videotape: *Digging Up Dinosaurs*
You may wish to show the videotape *Digging Up Dinosaurs* after using Activity Card C9 to reinforce the concept that living animals have characteristics similar to dinosaurs. Encourage children to name other living animals with characteristics similar to dinosaurs.

Using the ACTIVITY CARD

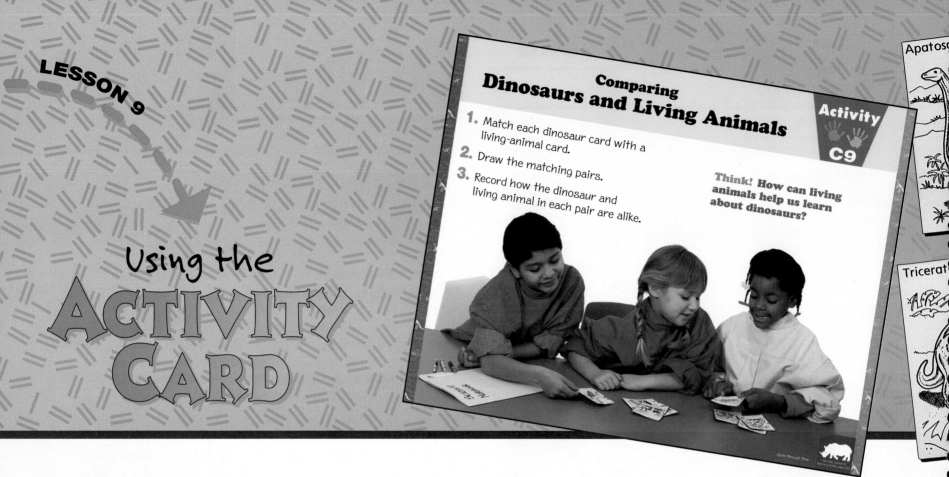

Comparing
Dinosaurs and Living Animals

Activity C9

1. Match each dinosaur card with a living-animal card.
2. Draw the matching pairs.
3. Record how the dinosaur and living animal in each pair are alike.

Think! How can living animals help us learn about dinosaurs?

Apatosau

Tricerat

Organize

Objective
- **Compare** dinosaurs with living animals.

Process Skills
- **Classify** dinosaurs and living animals according to similar characteristics.
- **Infer** how dinosaurs used their body parts, based on how living animals use their body parts.

Pacing: 20 minutes

Grouping: Small groups of 3–4

Materials
- Activity Card C9
- Dinosaur Cards
- Living-Animal Cards
- *Science Notebook* p. C25

For Best Results: Have children identify the living animals and tell what they know about them.

Guide

- **Warm-Up** Before children start the activity, have them identify the cards as animals alive today or as dinosaurs. Ask: **Have you ever seen a dinosaur? Would you like to see one?** Make certain that children understand that dinosaurs died off—or became **extinct**—about 65 million years ago. Allow them to express their reasons why they would or would not like to see a dinosaur.
- In step 1, ask: **Which dinosaur has a body part that looks somewhat like a body part of one of the living animals?** (If children have difficulty answering, point out distinctive body parts of the living animals, such as a long neck or horns. Have children compare that body part with each dinosaur until all pairs are matched.) *(classify)*
- In step 2, give children time to draw each matching pair in their *Science Notebooks.* If the activity takes too long, let them draw or trace the similar body parts only.
- In step 3, help children identify the similar body parts.

Responding To Individual Needs

Gifted and Talented Children Allow children to use reference books to learn where living animals shown on the Living-Animal Cards live, what they eat, and how they protect themselves. Ask children to report their findings to the class, perhaps using visual aids to assist them with their presentation.

Giraffe

Tyrannosaurus

Tiger

Rhinoceros

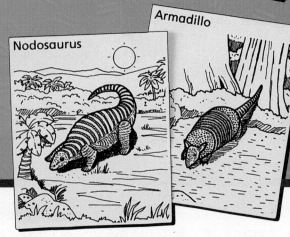

Nodosaurus

Armadillo

Close

- Review with children the similar body parts they observed on the living animals and the dinosaurs. Ask them to describe how the living animals use those body parts. Then have them speculate how the dinosaurs used similar parts. Lead them to *infer* that dinosaurs used similar parts in similar ways.

- **Think!** Answer: Body parts of living animals and dinosaurs that are alike could have had the same uses; such as horns for protection or long necks to reach the tops of trees.

- **Extend the Activity** Show children Poster Book page C1 from Lesson 1. Ask them to point out body parts on the dinosaurs that are similar to those found on animals alive today. Have children explain how they think the dinosaurs used those body parts.

Assess PERFORMANCE

 Expected Results

- Did children observe the body parts of the dinosaurs and the animals living today?
- Did they match the dinosaurs and living animals by their similar body parts?
- Did they draw pictures that showed the similar body parts?

 Process Skills Checklist, Assessment Guide p. C68

Use the Process Skills Checklist to record children's performance.

- Did children *classify* living animals and dinosaurs according to similar characteristics?
- Did children *infer* how dinosaurs used their body parts?

Group Skills Checklist, Assessment Guide p. C69

Use the Group Skills Checklist to record children's performance.

- Did children *communicate clearly* similarities between dinosaurs and living animals?
- Did they *listen* to each other's observations?

Alternate Activity 🖐 USES LESS TIME

Pacing: 10 minutes
Grouping: Individual
Materials

- Copies of Activity Support blackline masters: Dinosaur Cards, Living-Animal Cards
- Scissors
- Glue
- Crayons or colored pencils
- Paper

Procedure

- Have children cut out the cards. Ask them to compare the body parts of the dinosaurs and the living animals.

- Tell children to match each dinosaur with a living animal that has a similar body part and to glue the matching cards next to each other in two columns on a sheet of paper.

- For each pair of matching cards, have children color the similar body parts.

- Discuss with children how the animals living today use the colored body parts. (Long neck for getting food from trees, horns for protection). Ask children to speculate on how the dinosaurs used similar body parts. (Children should recognize that dinosaurs probably used similar body parts in similar ways.)

LESSON 9

Using the
POSTER BOOK & PICTURE CARDS

Dinosaurs became extinct a long time ago.
These birds are in danger of becoming extinct.
How can people prevent an animal from becoming extinct?

Use with Lesson 9, Teaching Guide page C84.

Earth Through Time C9

POSTER BOOK PAGE

Organize

Objective
- **Conclude** that some animals alive today are in danger of becoming extinct.

Process Skills
- **Infer** what might cause an animal to become endangered and how people might prevent an endangered animal from becoming extinct.
- **Classify** animals as endangered or extinct.

Pacing: 20 minutes

Grouping: Whole class

Materials
- Poster Book p. C9
- Picture Cards C16, C17, C18, C19, C20, C21, C22
  (See backs of Picture Cards for questions, facts, and related activities.)

Using the Student Edition: You may wish to use Student Edition pages C22–C23 to extend or replace the Poster Book lesson.

Guide
➊ Feeding a baby macaw
➋ Examining a baby macaw
➌ Scarlet Macaws

- **Warm-Up** Display Poster Book page C9. Write *endangered* on the chalkboard and ask children to find a word within the word. After they identify "danger," ask: **What do you think an endangered animal is?** (Children might respond that it is an animal that is in some kind of danger.) Explain that an **endangered** animal is in danger of dying off or becoming **extinct.**
- **Poster Book** Read the first sentence on the Poster Book page. Have children recall possible reasons why dinosaurs became extinct. (The climate changed, and the dinosaurs couldn't get enough food.)
- Read the second sentence. Lead children to recognize that the Scarlet Macaw is an endangered animal. Ask children to speculate why the macaw is endangered. (No suitable place to live; not enough food) *(infer)*
- Discuss with children how people can prevent endangered animals from becoming extinct. (Protect the animal from being hunted and killed and from having its environment destroyed.) *(infer)*
- **Picture Cards** After the class goes over the information on the backs of the cards, have children *classify* the animals as extinct or endangered.

🧍 Responding To Individual Needs

Children Acquiring English Proficiency   Help children find out the words for *extinct* and *endangered* in their native languages. Ask them to write the words and their definitions both in English and in their native language. Then have them work with a partner as they use the English words to classify the animals on the Picture Cards.

C16: Great Auk
C17: Passenger Pigeon
C18: Quagga
C19: Dodo
C20: Giant Panda
C21: Bengal Tiger
C22: Black Rhinoceros

Close

 Ask: **Are animals in more or in less danger of becoming extinct now that there are humans on the earth? Why?** (Help children conclude that humans can kill animals and destroy things in their environments so some animals can't find enough food or shelter.)

- **Extend the Activity** Have children choose an animal and explain how humans might be affected if the animal became extinct. In the **multi-age classroom**, you may wish to have some children write reports on extinct and endangered animals. Have them share their reports with the class.

 Concept Checklist, Assessment Guide p. C79

Use the Concept Checklist to record children's understanding.

- Do children recognize that some dinosaurs had characteristics similar to animals alive today?
- Do they understand the difference between an extinct animal and an endangered animal?

 Lesson Assessment, Assessment Guide p. C56

Use the Lesson 9 Assessment to evaluate children's understanding of the lesson concept.

 Debate

Ask children to describe a zoo. Explain that some people are against zoos and some people like zoos. Have children debate whether zoos are good or bad by telling how zoos help animals and how they hurt animals. (Zoos let people see animals; they feed and take good care of them; they breed them so they won't become extinct. Zoos also make animals live in small areas without their freedom.)

Science & Social Studies

SHARING IDEAS At one time Lake Erie was considered a "dead" lake. People made the water so dirty that nothing could live in it. Now people are cleaning up lakes and rivers so plants and animals can live there. Promote discussion by asking the following: **Why is clean water important to people? Why is it important to keep the animals in lakes and rivers alive? How can children help keep rivers and lakes clean?**

Science & Language Arts

WRITING AN ESSAY Have children choose an animal and write an essay that conveys why they don't want that animal to become extinct. They could begin the first paragraph with *The animal I would miss most is the (name)* and describe what they like about the animal. The second paragraph could begin *I do not want the animal to become extinct because_____.* In the paragraph, they should give reasons for their opinions.

INVESTIGATE FURTHER

UNIT PROJECT LINK

Dinosaur Place: Comparing Animals

Have children each draw on the Unit Project page a dinosaur and a living animal with a similar characteristic. Tell them to identify the animals and the characteristic that is similar. Encourage children to mount their drawings on construction paper and then display the drawings around the classroom.

When the Dinosaur Place exhibit is completed, invite children from other classes to visit it.

Use Unit Project page C101 in the Teacher Resource Book with this activity.

In the Science Center

Investigating Extinct and Endangered Animals

Objective
- **Conclude** that some animals alive today are in danger of becoming extinct.

Process Skills
- **Infer** how people can prevent the extinction of animals.
- **Communicate** how people can prevent the extinction of animals.

Pacing: 15 minutes

Grouping: Pairs

Materials
- Picture Cards C16, C17, C18, C19, C20, C21, C22
- Drawing paper
- Crayons or colored pencils

Procedure
- Invite each child to choose two Picture Cards. Have children read the questions on the backs of the cards to their partners, who answer the questions.
- Give time for the children to discuss the causes of the animals' extinction or endangerment. Then help them summarize reasons why animals become extinct and suggest things people can do to protect animals. *(infer)*
- Have children each select an endangered animal and draw a picture showing what can be done to help prevent the extinction of that animal. *(communicate)*

 Review the *Science Notebook*

Ask questions to see whether children remember and understand that some dinosaurs were similar to some animals alive today.

 Return to Baseline Assessment

Display children's responses to the Assess Prior Knowlege questions and read them aloud. Let children change or add information to reflect what they learned in the lesson.

 Discussion Starters

Ask children what they think might have caused dinosaurs to become extinct. (Possibility: an asteroid hit the earth, throwing tons of particles into the air, blocking out the sunlight and causing the earth to become colder. As a result, many plants died, and plant-eating dinosaurs did not get enough food. When the plant-eating dinosaurs died, the meat-eating dinosaurs that fed on those dinosaurs also died.)

 Debate

Present topics such as these for debate: **People should limit how many animals a hunter can kill; people should not build homes or shopping malls in areas where endangered animals live.**

Have children save their work for the portfolio selection process at the end of the unit.

Home-School Connection

The Explore at Home activity "Living in a Zoo" (Teacher Resource Book page C12) invites children to draw a picture of an endangered animal living in a zoo. After children have done the activity with their families and have brought in their drawings and sentences, invite them to share their discoveries with the class.

The family letter that ends the unit (Teacher Resource Book page C13) recommends additional activites the family can do together and books they may want to read together.

Science & Art

MAKING A COLLAGE

Explain that on some nature hunts, people "shoot" animals with cameras instead of guns. Ask children to draw or bring in pictures of animals that they don't want to become endangered or extinct. Mount the pictures on a bulletin board display titled "Our Animal Friends."

Portfolio Selection

Have children review their work from the unit and select pieces to include in their portfolios. See the portfolio assessment overview in the Assessment Guide for suggestions about how to use portfolio assessment in your classroom. You may wish to use the Inside My Science Portfolio page to help children make selections.

Unit Test

To assess children's understanding of specific science concepts, you may wish to give them the unit test in the Assessment Guide. See the unit test overview for a description of how unit tests are tailored to fit each level of reading readiness.

You may wish to use one or more of the following assessment options to evaluate students' understanding of the skills and concepts taught in this unit. These pages appear in the Teacher Resource Book.

Performance Assessment

The Performance Assessment for this unit, found on pages C62–C64, assists you in **evaluating how well children apply their scientific knowledge and skills.**

Use the Teacher Support (page C62) to guide you as you prepare to administer the Performance Assessment. Make copies of the Recording Page (page C63) for children to use as they complete the assessment. Use the Checklist (page C64) to record your evaluation of children's performance.

Unit Test

The Unit Test, on pages C90–C93, provides an instrument for **evaluating children's understanding of the unit concepts.** Each test includes a carefully designed mixture of objective questions and art to assess each lesson concept.

The Unit Test is tailored to a Second Grade level of reading readiness; all questions and instructions are directed to the child. Children are asked to write or draw their answers. Suggested answers to the questions on this test appear on page C94.

Portfolio Assessment

Help children choose for their portfolios a designated number of items that show progress in understanding concepts and using science process skills. Some suggestions for selecting items appear on page C81. Then **have each child identify his or her favorite work** on a copy of "Inside My Science Portfolio," a self-evaluation sheet on page C83.

For each child, use a copy of the Science Portfolio Evaluation Sheet on page C84 **to record how the contents of his or her portfolio demonstrate growth.** Include this evaluation sheet in each child's portfolio for use during family conferences.

Unit C Review

Student Edition pages C24–C25

Word Power
A. a. fossil remains   **b.** fossil imprint

B. 1. skull   **2.** pointed teeth
   3. skeleton   **4.** dinosaurs
   5. flat teeth   **6.** endangered
   7. fossils   **8.** extinct

Using Science Ideas
Because it had pointed teeth, it probably ate meat. Because its front legs were very small, it probably walked on two legs.

Solving Science Problems
1. Remains are a part of a real plant or animal. An imprint is not an actual part but a mark left when the plant or animal was pressed into soft material such as mud, that later hardened.
2. By looking at skeletons, teeth, footprints
3. By protecting animal environments and food sources

UNIT PROJECT Wrap-Up

Before inviting other classes to visit the Dinosaur Place exhibit, assign each child a dinosaur for which they will be an "expert." Have children make name tags, with a picture of their dinosaur, that say, "Hi, I'm [name of child]. I am a [name of dinosaur] expert." Invite visitors to ask the "expert" questions.

After children complete the Unit Project, you may wish **to assess children's performance** by using the Unit Project Scoring Checklist on page C102 of the Teacher Resource Book.

MATERIALS LIST

Earth Through Time 2C

Materials	Quantity for 6 groups of 4	In Kit	C/NC*	Page
Activity Card C1	1		NC	C18
Activity Card C2	1		NC	C26
Activity Card C3	1		NC	C34
Activity Card C4	1		NC	C42
Activity Card C5	1		NC	C50
Activity Card C6	1		NC	C58
Activity Card C7	1		NC	C66
Activity Card C8	1		NC	C74
Activity Card C9	1		NC	C82
airtight container	6		NC	C50
blocks of wood (2" × 3" × ½")	12	✔	NC	C66
bones, plastic chicken	6 sets	✔	NC	C58
bones, plastic rat	6 sets	✔	NC	C58
cereal, dry	6 cups		C	C66
crayons or colored pencils	6 boxes		C	C74
dinosaur models with guide	2 sets	✔	NC	C18
dough compound	2 pkg	✔	C	C42
flour	15 lb		C	C50
fossil imprint of fern	6	✔	NC	C34
fossil imprint of leaf	6	✔	NC	C42
fossil remains of snail	6	✔	NC	C34
goggles	6	✔	NC	C42, C50, C58, C66
golf tees	2 pkg (20)	✔	NC	C66
hand lens	15	✔	NC	C18, C34, C42
measuring cup	1		NC	C50
mixing bowl, large	1		NC	C50
mixing spoon	1		NC	C50
newspapers	several copies		C	C58
once-living object (leaf)	6		C	C42
once-living object (shell)	6	✔	NC	C42
once-living object (twig)	6		C	C42
overhead projector	1		NC	C26
paper plates, large	1 pkg (30)	✔	C	C42, C50, C58
petroleum jelly (optional)	1		C	C50
plastic wrap	1		C	C50
ruler, 12"	6		NC	C50
salt	15 cups		C	C50
sand	six 5-lb bags	✔	C	C58
Science Notebook	24 copies		C	C18, C26, C34, C42, C50, C58, C66, C74, C82
spoons, plastic	12	✔	NC	C58
tape, transparent	6 rolls		C	C74
timer, 1-minute	6	✔	NC	C66
tray, foil	6	✔	NC	C58
tree leaves	12		C	C66
water	1 gallon		C	C50
yardstick	1		NC	C26

*C/NC = Consumable/Nonconsumable

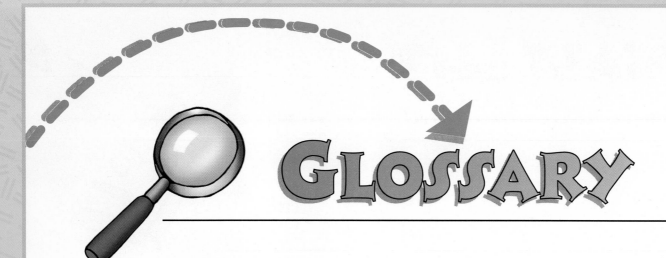

GLOSSARY

 C

Chasmosaurus (kaz mō sôr′əs) A dinosaur with a small nose horn, two larger horns above the brows, and a frill with large openings in its skeleton. (C75) Chasmosaurus was about 17 feet in length.

Compsognathus (cämp säg′nə thəs) One of the smallest known dinosaurs, no larger than a chicken. (C26) Compsognathus was only about 2½ feet in length. It may be an ancestor of the birds.

crush To break into fine pieces by grinding, pounding or pressing. (C66)

 D

dinosaur Now-extinct animal of the Mesozoic Era, which was from 225 to 65 million years ago. (C20) Some dinosaurs were probably cold-blooded and sluggish reptiles while others were like warm-blooded mammals. Some dinosaurs grew to enormous size.

 E

endangered In danger of dying off or becoming extinct. (C84) The giant panda is an endangered animal.

Euoplocephalus (yoo ō plə sef′ə ləs) A large ankylosaur with armored bands down its back and a bony tail club. (C75) Euoplocephalus was about 20 feet in length.

extinct No longer existing. (C82) Dinosaurs became extinct about 65 million years ago.

 F

flat teeth Blunt teeth that are good for grinding food. (C66) Many plant-eating dinosaurs had flat teeth.

footprint A track or impression made by a foot. (C52) Footprints give clues about the size of the person or animal that made them.

fossil imprints Marks formed when a plant or animal leaves a trace, or print, of itself in soil, which gradually turns to rock. (C42)

fossil remains What is left of a plant or animal that was once living long ago. (C58)

fossils Preserved evidence of former life. (C34) Fossils can either be imprints, which show what is left when a plant or animal is pressed against something, or the actual remains of a plant or animal.

 G

grind To crush into bits. (C66)

handprint A mark or impression made by a hand. (C50) Handprints give clues about the size of the person or animal that made them.

imprints Marks made by pressure. (C34)

Lambeosaurus (lam bē ō sôr′əs) A duck-billed dinosaur with a large crest shaped like a hatchet blade. (C28) Lambeosaurus was about 50 feet in length.

model A representation or miniature replica of something. (C20)

pointed teeth Sharp teeth that are good for tearing food. (C66) Many meat-eating dinosaurs had pointed teeth.

remains What is left of something. (C34)

reptile Any of a group of vertebrates that are cold-blooded, breathe air, and usually have skin covered with scales or bony plates. (C20) Snakes, lizards, turtles, and alligators are reptiles.

skeleton The framework of bones and cartilage in vertebrates. (C74) The skeleton supports the muscles and supports and protects the body's organs.

skull The case of bone or cartilage that forms most of the skeleton of the head. (C66) The skull encloses the brain and supports the jaws.

Stegosaurus (steg ə sôr′əs) A herbivorous dinosaur with heavy, bony armor in the form of plates and spikes along the back and tail. (C26) Stegosaurus was up to 30 feet in length.

Styracosaurus (stī räk′ ō sôr′əs) Dinosaur with a huge horn on its snout, two small horns above the eyes and a frill that ended in small spikes. (C26) Styracosaurus was about 18 feet in length.

tear To pull apart by force. (C66)

Triceratops (trī ser′ə täps) A dinosaur with a large horn above each eye and a smaller horn on the nose, a bony collar extending from the neck and a long and powerful tail. (C28) Triceratops was about 25–30 feet in length.

Velociraptor (və läs′ə rap tər) A small but fierce two-legged dinosaur with large claws on its small hands which it used for grasping prey. (C28) Velociraptor was about 6–7 feet in length.

INDEX

CREDITS

Front Cover: *Photography:* Jade Albert; *Photography Production:* Picture It Corporation; *Illustration:* Doreen Gay-Kassel.

Contributing Artists: Nancy Tobin: C11; Terry Boles: C13; Richard Courtney: C17.

Photographs
All photographs by Silver Burdett Ginn (SBG) unless otherwise noted.

C8: *t.* Vertebrate Paleontology/Royal Ontario Museum; *b.l.* ©John Mitchell/Photo Researchers, Inc.; *b.r.* Breck P. Kent. C8–C9: *bkgd* Dinamation International Society; *border* Scott Brenner/The Stock Shop/Medichrome. C19: Grant Huntington for SBG. C25: ©Francois Gohier/Photo Researchers, Inc. C33: Tom Bean/DRK Photo. C35: Grant Huntington for SBG. C41: Breck P. Kent. C43: Grant Huntington for SBG. C49: ©Francois Gohier/Photo Researchers, Inc. C51: Grant Huntington for SBG. C57: Phil Degginger/Color-Pic, Inc. C59: Grant Huntington for SBG. C65: John Eastcott/VVA Momatiuk/DRK Photo. C67: Grant Huntington for SBG. C73: E.R. Degginger/Color-Pic, Inc. C81: *l.* Larry Tackett/Tom Stack & Associates; *m.t.* Kennan Ward/DRK Photo; *m.b.* Barbara Von Hoffman/Tom Stack & Associates; *t.r.* Rod Planck/Tom Stack & Associates; *b.r.* Dave E. Fleetham/Tom Stack & Associates.